"Mamas Gotta Grow! lifts ⁊.
Inside you will find stories i g
of the female spirit. As yc x
journeys, you will come to see that while often in different directions,
turns and speeds, the map of both womanhood and motherhood truly
weave us together."

- Michelle Emmick - Editor-in-Chief, Ask Us Beauty Magazine
ig: @askusbeautymagazine

"I read this book in bed, in pyjamas, hair in a messy bun while sipping
on some wine and eating chocolate. This book was the perfect pairing
for some 'me time'. It is incredibly relatable and enjoyable. Having so
many personalities involved keeps the book interesting the whole way
through. I can't wait to read it again!"

- Sacha Welsh - CHC Founder, Welsh Wellness, Mother of Three
www.welshwellness.com I ig: @welsh_wellness
tiktok: @sachawelshwellness I fb: welshwellness I yt: welshwellness

"Mamas Gotta Grow! is a light hearted, wonderful read for any mom
in any season of motherhood. It is also easy to read, and keeps the
reader's attention by introducing new women and experiences. It's
refreshing to hear from honest, relatable women who are going through
similar situations. Motherhood is a journey and this book wholeheartedly
exemplifies that!"

- Lindsay Fossee - Full-time Mama of Four I ig: @thesparklymomof4

"Deep insights, wisdom and inspiration on every page. Through vulnerable
real life examples, Mama's Gotta Grow! helps moms reconnect with
themselves, find their inner strength to overcome challenges, and move
towards their highest potential. Mama's Gotta Grow! is a must read for
any mom who doesn't just want to survive, but flourish through these
uncertain times."

- Marcia Miatke - Executive and Women's Coach, Mother of Two
ig: @marciamiatke @empoweredwomansacademy

"Mama's Gotta Grow! is a powerful collection of stories by twenty incredible women that showcases their individual experiences, perspective and lessons learned. It takes you on an inspirational journey towards finding balance, happiness, and community in knowing you are not alone in the ebbs and flows of life and motherhood. No matter where you are in your journey, you will benefit from the vulnerability, courage, and messages shared with each magical story."

- Natalie James - Multipassionate Entrepreneur and Podcast Host, Mother of Three | www.imnataliejames.com
ig: @im.nataliejames | ig: @pivotandpolishpodcast

"As a daughter, a sister, and now a mother to two beautiful girls, reading this book touched me in every way. This is an amazing read for any woman. Looking through the various stories allowed me to learn that I am not alone in this world. We all come across surprising obstacles and paths throughout motherhood. The best we can do is keep our heads up and do our best. Amazing read!"

- Roya N. - Business Owner, Mother of Two | ig: @momstop.to

"The courage in vulnerability from these mamas is truly motivating! Hearing everyone speak their unique truth is both captivating and inspiring following unprecedented times. As someone who supports women, 'adapting to change' is profound. This book is a must read for anyone who feels the significance of motherhood."

- Jess Thomson - Certified Labour and Postpartum Doula
www.doulajessthomson.com | ig: @doulajessthomson

"Who knew reproduction would be so complex. Who knew a new title would be so life altering. Mom. Can we 'have it all?' Why do we feel such judgement? Is there such a thing as balance? Will we ever be the same person again? There is so much to process in our motherhood journey by slowing down; reading this book is the perfect way to start."

- Koreena (Singh) Johnson - Giving Sundays
www.givingsundays.com | ig: @givingsundays

"Us mamas can get so caught up in everything, we forget about 'me' time. This book has helped me with the finer things in life."

- Moms N Dumbbells - Subscription Box
www.momsndumbbells.com | ig: @momsndumbbells

Foreword by Tova Leigh
Best-Selling Author of *F*cked at 40,* and *You Did WHAT?*

mama's Gotta Grow!

Inspiring Conscious Growth in Motherhood;
Pandemic Pivoting, Adapting to Change,
Shifting Lifestyles, and Embracing New Normals.

Co-Authored by:
Krysta Lee | Sally Lovelock | Stephanie Barkley-Bequette
Pina Crispo | Whitney Stout | Leanne Sigrist | Elizabeth Meekes
Candace Clark Trinchieri | Emanuela Martina Hall | Lisa Kern
Jaime Hayes & Marnie VandenBroek-Hookey | Jessi Harris
Susan Elstob | Sandy Casella | Abby Creek | Angel Kibble
Teresa Sturino Schiavone | Sonia Dong | Tamara Trotman

Published in Canada for Global Distribution by Golden Brick Road Publishing House Inc. Printed in North America.

Handwritten font created by: Jayden Ware

Paperback ISBN: 9781989819142 | ebook ISBN: 9781989819159

Media: hello@gbrph.ca

Book orders: orders@gbrph.ca

Contents

Section 3
Shifting Lifestyles: Conscious Choices

Section 4
Embracing New Normals: Growing Forward

Foreword

Tova Leigh
Best-Selling Author of *F*cked at 40*, and *You Did WHAT?*

Anytime amazing women collaborate, it's going to be my cup of tea! I absolutely *loved* the first book, *Mama's Gotta Work!*, and was so happy to hear there was going to be a sequel.

Mama's Gotta Grow! delves into every aspect of being a mom: the good, the bad, and the not-so-talked-about (but should-be-talked-about) moments. I loved the reflection on Covid-19, which affected so many lives, women's in particular.

As women and mothers, we often miss that sense of community and connection. I think this book gives the reader that feeling of not being alone—of being part of something bigger—in the most comforting way.

While learning from experts like some of the authors in this book is great, there is also a lot of value in learning from your peers, fellow moms who are in the trenches with you, and those who have stories to tell with insights from their own experiences. I found these individual stories to be honest, revealing, and even challenging at times—but in a good way. It's fantastic to get such a compelling array of voices and different perspectives.

I think this book will provide hope and inspiration for many women and mothers out there. A job well done, ladies, and a fabulous book all around!

-Tova Leigh

www.tovaleigh.com

ig: @tova_leigh

tiktok: @tova_leigh

fb: @mythoughtsaboutstuff

Introduction

Dearest Mama,

Welcome! As you journey along your path of growth through motherhood, we invite you to take some time for yourself and indulge in the stories shared here from mothers just like you. We are a sisterhood of twenty-one mamas from across North America. Collectively we have fifty children, and we come from many different backgrounds, professions, ages, stages, family dynamics, religions, and beliefs. We vary in experience from thirty to sixty years of life on earth, in different stages of motherhood, and with children of different ages from newborn to adult. One of the many things that unites us here with you is the calling to speak our truth and share our stories—with hopes it will shine a light on the divine mother within you.

We wish to extend our open hands and hearts to you and embrace you as part of this community—with compassion, love, and support. We know the journey through motherhood is not an easy one, and with the way the world has recently taken a turn through unprecedented times, it's more important now than ever before to come together and hold space for one another. It takes a village, and with so many mamas feeling as though they're falling without the support of a sisterhood, we're making this village virtual—and we're inviting you to come along for the ride.

Motherhood is more enjoyable when we grow with the ebbs and flows of life.

The ups and downs that make up the life of a mother are easier to navigate with the gentle guidance, loving ears, and kind mouths of the women who walk the path alongside us and before us. We consciously chose to dig deeply and reveal some of our innermost wisdoms and takeaways, and we invite you to take whatever you need to add to your toolkit. Whether you're a brand-new mama, or a beautifully seasoned one, there is something here for you, and we honor you and whatever part of the path you're on.

We are here to inform you—you're never alone. Although the gift of being a mother can sometimes feel inclusive of challenges too great to bear, we wish to remind you that you are a sovereign being, and you carry within you an incredibly powerful gift simply by existing. You have access to invaluable knowledge within the pages of this book, which details various situations, complications, and celebrations worth sharing!

The collection of stories was carefully crafted with love, in hopes of inspiring, encouraging, and uplifting you—with all the feels.

It takes courage to show up and be vulnerable enough to grow—this is not lost on us—so we commend you for being here. Thank you for consciously choosing to open your mind to the possibilities that are out there waiting for you. Whatever situation you may currently find yourself in, please know this is a judgment-free zone, and a safe space to lean into. We see you, we hear you, and we feel you. We get it, mama, and we've got you!

Grab yourself a cuppa tea, joe, or jack—whatever floats your fancy! Put on (or stay in) your comfies, grab some snacks, then please sit back and relax as we take you along on quests of self-discovery, bravery, and breakthroughs in growth through motherhood.

You deserve all the love, appreciation, and gratitude this world has to offer, and now it's your turn to grow, mama, grow!

With love, light, and blessings,

-Krysta Lee

Section One

Pandemic Pivoting:
2020 Vision

*"Mothers are the pivot on which the family spins,
Mothers are the pivot on which the world spins."*

~ Pam Brown

FEATURING:

Sally Lovelock
Stephanie Barkley-Bequette
Pina Crispo
Whitney Stout
Leanne Sigrist

.

Chapter One

Juggling Through This Single Mum Circus

"Your circus is not your failure,
it's the entertainment in your story."

Sally Lovelock

SALLY LOVELOCK

www.althorpmontessorischool.com
ig: @sally.lovelock | @althorp_montessori-school

Sally Lovelock was born in Midland, Ontario in 1974 and moved to Burlington at the age of two. Sally attended M.M. Robinson High School where she met her lifelong friends who would personify the meaning of friendship. Sally moved to England in 1995 to care for her father, who later passed away from brain cancer. While living in a small village in the country, Sally discovered the Montessori philosophy and enrolled in college at Montessori Centre International. She later went on to open her own school in 2007: Althorp Montessori School. This journey has brought Sally physical, emotional, mental, and spiritual growth. Her goal is to reach as many early year educators and parents as possible to convey the importance of the absorbent mind from birth to age six, and how we can guide these little leaders on a path to make a big impact on our Earth.

Now living in the Niagara Region in Ontario, Canada, Sally credits her Reiki certificate for helping her find inner peace and balance while juggling her Montessori School and her two extraordinary boys.

Juggling Through This Single Mum Circus

I'm twenty years old, walking up Oxford Street, on my way to Marks and Spencer's to grab my lunch. The London air is warm, the spring flowers are already in bloom; there's no need for a jacket. I remember it like it was yesterday: my single life as a casino croupier, working at Hyde Park Corner. I wore an evening gown to work and piled on the makeup for this glamorous job at a private casino. My only stress was pushing my way through all the London tourists at the tube station to catch my connecting train back to my small village life. Getting to the gym was the last thing on my mind. My single life was all about meeting up at the local pub or the local football club where everyone knew me by name. This village felt like home, and I believed that this was where my future would be.

Fast-forward twenty-six years, here I am in Canada waking up with a knee in my back, a pain in my neck, and a headache. Single again, but this time I'm a single mum of two boys, aged eight and ten, who still love to co-sleep with their mama. Now I hop out of bed, jump in the shower, make breakfast, prepare school lunches, and have replaced that evening gown with a business suit. My evening workout has now become my time for me—it has become my clarity.

After spending eighteen years with the father of my children, we went our separate ways. We may be the same people, but with life-changing experiences we have new growth, and this change needs to be acknowledged. My small village life is now just a few days to escape when I can find time to hop on an airplane. Today, we own our growth as we welcome a new norm to our family of three.

My focus is on maintaining a healthy co-parenting relationship with my ex-husband. As an early childhood educator, I have witnessed many separations and the role the parents play in offering security for their children while transitioning to their new routine. My goal was building a new relationship with the father of my children, one that showed my children love and respect. I needed to let go of control and allow my ex-husband to shine—my boys need him just as much as they need me. Our parenting style is definitely different, but my children will always see us united. For us this includes having their dad (and the dog) over for dinner every now and then.

With healthy boundaries there is no need for conflict, the point in moving forward is to offer a happier home environment.

At times you need to stop and take a deep breath, look at your child's face, and understand their smile is worth every minute of building mutual respect as a family living in two different homes. The next obstacle would be an unfamiliar step, as we find balance while navigating, bringing new partners into our family dynamic. We had no idea what this would look like and relied on the children to guide us with their comfort levels around these well-planned-out family conversations.

Change is healthy because as we go through many identity transitions, we rediscover ourselves. There are so many lessons along the way, and for me, opening up to dating in 2020 has probably been the biggest eye-opener. It's like getting on a bike after years of not riding one, right? Wrong. The truth is, it's a circus—and the ride is extremely entertaining. With social media, online dating, and texting, you'll learn new lingo like "ghosting" and "benching." Remember when young men would have the courage to phone you and ask you out on a date? This has been replaced with photos. Sure, selfies can be cute, but let's keep them PG—for some of you, I'm old enough to be your mom! And seriously, who has time for decoding emojis?! A simple conversation is like pulling teeth in 2020!

After my marriage ended, I entered a transition of rediscovering myself. It was a scary time, and took courage to battle through the guilt of separation. I thought I was alone; it took me over a year to discover that my growth included my two boys, and that their growth included me. I did not need a partner; I was a strong, independent woman leading the way with two very observant young men at my side—listening to my words and watching my every move.

I knew that my actions were setting the foundation on which my boys would enter manhood.

My biggest mistake was also my biggest escape. Three months after my marriage ended, I should have been finding clarity and embracing my new freedom. Instead, I found myself in a year-long toxic relationship, one in which I could not experience healthy growth, as his character traits somehow became a reflection of my new identity. If I had entered this relationship today, it would have lasted two weeks. My boys witnessed my vulnerability, and it was with this experience that I recognized the importance in sharing this part of my life with my children. Keeping them in the dark was the last thing they needed. They needed to understand the process of watching me fall and rise. Running (as fast as I could) from this relationship was the start to many lessons on choosing a partner. My checklist was clear, and I knew exactly what I didn't want in a man. It was time to open myself to what I did want. Becoming self-aware as a newly single mama was the greatest gift to myself. What I saw as red flags, were now stored safely in my memory bank, ready to guide me on this next path.

Stepping forward after the challenges of juggling a failed marriage, to a toxic relationship, and dating in a pandemic—I needed to ask myself what my expectations were in a partner, and the role he would play in my boys' lives. I am self-sufficient; I am not looking for someone to be my provider. My boys have an amazing father, they do not need someone to parent them. I know this man will be a bonus to our family of three, bringing love and fun times to our home. Not needing a father figure, this man will be their friend. He will show my boys how much he adores their mother; witnessing this love is all they will need. My boys and I will not settle for anything less; we are deserving and worthy of the fairy tale. My job is to let down my walls, and allow this man to find his way. My boys will observe this relationship and take from it what they need on their journey in finding a future partner.

The journey to this point has had its ups and downs.

The ups were mostly the laughs I shared with my girlfriends as they would ask about my dating life—these games were all new to me at forty-five. There were guys who had never been married and had no kids, and the struggle was finding compatibility and common ground—as we had taken different directions in our lives. Could they ever appreciate all of me? That being mama is one of my greatest successes? Would they recognize that my time without my children was likely already taken up by running errands, me time, and girlfriend time—so offering them one night a week was their opportunity to step up?! These guys ended up being the guys that have no clue you are aware of them stalking you on social media.

I would sit and listen to the girls talking about their online dating experiences. Of course, some couples do meet this way, but for me I only lasted three dates. I felt like I was the juggling act in my own circus! It was all about keeping up with who was who, and remembering what guy you were talking to. Apparently, this is called "serial dating." Going through profiles and passing judgments on appearances as you swipe; passing the shirtless, goateed, pierced, cat-loving, smoking men taking selfies in their sports cars. All while being faced with the challenge of dating during the global pandemic brought on by COVID-19! Meeting at a coffee shop or for a walk with our face masks on was about as exciting as dating was going to get.

One afternoon, I sat across from a guy, and I was wearing my school's gym clothes (I'm that "keeping it real on the first date equals casual clothes" kind of woman). He lost me about two minutes into the conversation, yet I sat there for another two hours thinking *how do I end this date?* He went on and on about his designer clothes, buying his mum a three-thousand-dollar purse, looking for a house worth two million dollars, and how he was going to trade his Mercedes in for a Porsche. Clearly, he misread my yoga pants and jean jacket approach, and mistook me for a woman looking for a three-carat diamond ring. The best laugh was out loud, in my car, as he revved his car engine and sped past me on the highway after our date ended. Yes, he thought it went well, and asked for another date . . . *really?!*

I learned dating during a pandemic wasn't going to work for me. When all you can do is meet for a walk—never seeing each other's smile, or full expression due to masks—connecting on a real level is so much harder. No doubt it was a part of my dating experience that needed to be explored—I'll take from it a few laughs, and maybe even a lesson learned.

> *I have worked hard at keeping myself mentally strong through this pandemic so that I can offer my strength to my children, my staff, and the students at the Montessori School.*

There were days when I was alone making the biggest business decisions of my life. There were days when I wanted to scrap my boys' online learning and homeschool them myself. There were days when the entire weight of the world was consuming every part of me, and the responsibility almost broke me, but I knew it was in me to find peace in the craziness of this world. Too many people needed me, and giving in to weakness has never been an option for me.

I turned off the news, I blocked negative people on social media, and cleared my mind of the poor influences around me. It is what it is; I cannot heal the world, but I can work on my own mindset and be present for the people around me. Yes, a partner would have been nice to fall on at this time, but the power of pulling through this craziness alone would only add fire to my independence! My truth is that I have always believed in the power of energy and the universe bringing us what we need, at the time it is right for us. When we find contentment with who we are, and close the doors to drama, we open space for what has been waiting for us all along.

Unexpected, would be how I describe what has happened; today I find myself living the story of a Hallmark Christmas movie—you know those stories that only exist on TV, the ones that make you roll your eyes even as you are grabbing a tissue to wipe the tears? Apparently, it all started in grade six on the school bus; little did I know back then, there was a boy who had a crush on me. He waited at my bus stop with me. This same boy would steal my heart in ninth grade with a simple smile and the cutest lisp ever. He even took the city bus all the way to the hospital at fourteen years of age to see me when I broke my femur. Of course, no high school relationship is going to survive three months in a body cast, but we did cross paths many times in high school and remained friends.

Fast forward, this time by thirty-five years, and his grin has been able to melt my heart all over again. This time, life experiences have prepared us for a second chance at love. Replace the city bus ride to the hospital with a three-hour shuttle from Invermere to Calgary, an eight-hour wait at the airport, and an overnight journey from British Columbia to Ontario for a New Year's Eve date. My boys see his name on my phone every day when he calls, they have heard his voice over the speaker in the car—this is something new to them. They know that their mummy will only allow this man into the conversation when the timing is right for them. We, as a unit, understand that this is not about me or about him, this is about us—and blending these relationships should be a natural process.

I am happy on my own, in my own space. Me-time is a gift to my soul. My family of three brings me happiness. However, I also recognize that as I let down my walls and breathe in as I listen to his words—*"this is the way"*—I am accepting a bonus-love that changes our family of three to a family of six. Change can be scary, but also exciting! Losing control does not mean I have lost sight of where I am going. When we take things one day at a time, and understand things will not be perfect, we can have a realistic approach to the craziness that the blending of our families will be.

Together we can grow and create a whole
new circus.

What is your role in your family dynamic, and how can you find it after separation? A failed relationship is about two people coming to the conclusion that they no longer work together; it is showing courage to your children that you can own the role you play in their lives. Be aware of the false family façades you see on social media, and do not allow them to hold any power over the role you need to play in your child's life. Stay focused on reality; fear can alter our mindset. Opening the doors to growth and accepting change is acknowledging your right to a second chance at love. Whether you are seeking happiness, peace, or love, it will only come to you once you have found clarity. Your path has a plan, it will guide you through your own circus, and teach you many lessons as you grow.

Chapter Two

The Spiral

"Make like a tree and: stay grounded,
connect with your roots, turn over a new
leaf, honor your natural beauty,
keep growing."

Stephanie Barkley-Bequette

STEPHANIE BARKLEY-BEQUETTE

ig: @Roamward.Bound | fb: @TheRoamschoolBus
TikTok: @RoamwardBound | yt: www.youtube.com/roamwardbound

Steph's religion is love. Her faith is in the rise and fall of the tides, the wind beneath her wings, the roots that she transpires from, and the fire in her soul. Her practice as a certified Yoga trainer, Reiki healer, writer, artist, and mother includes incorporating Mother Earth's elements into her physicality, mentality, and spirituality. In tune with nature and the moon, she honors her seasons and cycles. She finds strength, inspiration, and balance in both the brightest of days, and darkest of nights. She and her husband, Erik, share a beautiful, blended family of six. The family's shared spontaneity and enthusiasm for exploration enticed them to buy a school bus in the early fall of 2020! They named her *Roam*, and are converting her into the tiny mobile home of their dreams. Much of their journey will be left open for the unknown, with an aim to leave their route flexible enough to *roam* new roads as they call out to them. The family is thankful to be able to bring their careers and education on the road, offering intuition a chance to navigate this schoolroom called life.

The Spiral

As I'm jotting notes for this chapter into my notebook, my nursing toddler kicked my *now cold* cup of *bold* chai all over the pages. Note taken: let's spill some *cold, hard* truth on motherhood, mindset, healing, and growth.

> *"If you don't make time for your wellness, you will be forced to make time for your illness."*
> *-Unknown*

I had been trying to outrun my shadows for over a decade. The darkness would never fail to catch up to me once a month. When it would dissipate, I'd spend the rest of the month trying to make up for the cancelled plans and overdue responsibilities left in its aftermath. It didn't take long to burn out from the overload, and too soon, the darkness would catch up to me again. I'd have no energy left to do anything but succumb to it, again.

After a decade of this cycle, I finally worked up the will to speak to a mental health specialist. I was diagnosed with bipolar disorder and introduced to antipsychotics on top of the antidepressants my doctor had prescribed to me years before. Although the meds did alleviate my initial issues, new (*worse*) symptoms were now manifesting from them that didn't sit right with my soul. To be brutally honest, my dependence on the tablets made me feel even less in control than ever before. Medication can be a balancing factor for many struggling with their mental health, however, the only real growth taking place for me was in my growing addiction to the prescriptions. *Addiction* is a devil I've watched my bloodline dance with before, and I know when history is at risk of repeating itself. It took strength to voice my concern when the majority of the support groups and professionals of Western culture claim that my diagnosis cannot go pharmacologically untreated. Every*body* reacts differently; you know yourself best. Trust your instincts.

I chose to take a different approach in regulating my mental health and wellness. I was tired of being faced with *fixed-mindset* advice that focused largely on physical prescriptions and failed to promote long-term mental, emotional, (and spiritual) development. Due to the COVID-19 pandemic, the opportunities for remote work and classes became more of a thing, so I now had a *flexible* and *affordable* opportunity to complete some of the therapies and programs I had been wanting to pursue as treatment alternatives. Accredited courses on cognitive behavioral therapy, and dialectical behavior therapy are now easily accessible and available to complete online. Thanks to my studies, new knowledge, and broader perspectives, I was able to expand my focus past trying to treat my symptoms (or on some days, deny them entirely), and begin a pursuit of healing the roots that manifested my symptoms in the first place. When I stopped trying to quiet my demons, I could listen closer to the underlying messages within their cries. The key is to find your balance and have the courage to walk the *golden brick road* lit up in your heart.

Transforming illness to wellness is not easy, no matter what road you take.

I found improvement when I stopped looking at my episodes as psychotic breaks, and instead embraced them as nodes to my growth. When we can identify what triggers us, we can identify what part of us needs healing. My mind had been perceiving my depression as a steep downward plunge of lows that I needed to chase highs to escape from. With the right shift in perspective, I now appreciate that growth isn't linear. Also, rather than seeing my life as a series of peaks and troughs on a timeline, I now visualize my journey as a spiral, continually coiling forward. A spiral in which we re-experience the things we thought we already understood or healed from; gaining deeper knowledge and personal development when we corkscrew through a layer. The only way out is *through*. My cycles became my teachers, instead of my tormentors.

Writing the word *corkscrew* without immediately feeling compelled to pop open a bottle, reassures me that my wounds are in fact healing, and I'm on the right path in my journey of self-discipline, self-love, and breaking destructive generational cycles.

Healing begins with shedding any limiting beliefs inherited via familial and cultural conditioning, while challenging the negativity bias in our brains that naturally emerges in infancy. The negativity bias is the idea that thoughts, emotions, and interactions of a more negative nature have a greater effect on one's subconscious than neutral or positive occurrences. For humankind, it is suggested that the positives do not naturally outweigh the negatives, having less of an impact on a person's cognition than something on the opposing end of the scale.[1] This was, and still is, a natural survival mechanism in all of us. You are not broken for battling with your mind; you are human. Although we no longer need to be on the same level of constant high alert as our early ancestors, the negativity bias is still wired in our brains today, heightening how we react and respond to what we perceive as threatening situations.

"The mind is like Velcro for negative experiences and Teflon for positive ones."
-Rick Hanson

Gradually shifting my natural outlook on life and establishing my own fundamental faith that isn't fueled by (or the fuel for) fear, I was able to see my "demons" (unregulated emotions, unprocessed trauma, and unhealthy thought processes) in a new light. Beneath the monstrous façade that I was swayed to perceive them as, they were not strange, unfamiliar, or frightening at all. They were the frightened, all-too-familiar parts of myself that I disconnected with anytime my body or psyche felt threatened. They weren't meaning to startle with their presence as they attempted to make their way back up to the surface, they were only reaching for some light, for a chance to bloom from the depths in which they had been buried. Instead of attempting to balance out an over-powering trait in myself, my ego would naturally blaspheme the whole quality into the abyss. I disconnected with many aspects of myself for a long time—including my creativity and passion due to negative experiences leaving me naïve and ridiculed when exploring these alleys. My shadows gradually brought all of my repressed traumas and shame up to the surface so that I could finally shed the needed light and compassion upon them to be brought to *balance*. Any time I would dismiss the chance to learn the lesson presenting itself, it would cycle back in a similar scenario down the road. *The spiral.*

"Sometimes when you're in a dark place you think you've been buried, but you've actually been planted." -Christine Caine

With a deconstruction of my former beliefs, a shift in mindset, and the willingness to face my demons, my *breakdowns* continue to lead me to

---

1 Kendra Cherry, "Why Our Brains Are Hardwired to Focus on the Negative," Verywell Mind, April 29, 2020, https://www.verywellmind.com/negative-bi-as-4589618#.

my greatest *breakthroughs*. There is a lesson in every hardship. I didn't believe that I was deserving of the kind of self-love that permitted my subconscious to do anything but doubt itself and remind me of my failures, but as we heal inward, we project less hurt outward onto ourselves (and others). Understanding our own darkness is the best method for understanding the darkness in others. Like with many fairy-tale villains, with compassion we can help the "*monsters*" in ourselves and others remember who they truly were before they were cast into the big-bad-wolf narrative. Hurt people *hurt people*. Healed people *heal people*.

> *"You now walk your inner wolf like a well-trained service dog; it no longer walks you."*
> -Linda Casselman

Humans have unlimited potential for adaptation and growth. We are constantly modifying our traits and behaviors in accordance to our beliefs and views. Our personal perspectives are also constantly shifting by the influence of our own intuition and experiences. When we identify ourselves with any set label (religious or political views, wealth, status, lifestyle, etc.), we are potentially restricting ourselves from personal development and adaptability. I'm personally super into astrology, but I try to be cautious when identifying as a Gemini, because the presumed "traits" can sometimes find me limiting my own capabilities and potential. As for my diagnosis, I haven't gone through years of exceptionally transforming and altering my body, mind, and soul (in motherhood alone) just to be tossed into a box and stamped with a label, when all I needed was to be granted a damn break from society's expectations and offered some knowledge of the right value.

As mothers, we witness the transformative potential of the human body and mind over and over again, day after day, year after year in ourselves, and in our children! Keep believing in your transformation and growth, in whatever area you're working on. What's impossible for others isn't necessarily impossible for you.

> *"Your ability to heal is greater than anyone has permitted you to believe."*
> -Unknown

I never used to grant myself time to recharge. In turn, I went into overdrive—spending energy I didn't have—trying to hide and deny that I was always depleted and running on fumes. I now allow myself to radiate, then retreat with the phases of the moon, instead of believing the natural process to be a *disorder* in my life. Like the moon, we must go through phases of emptiness to feel full again. Unapologetically stepping out of the light from time to time to process what the previous period had to teach me, is now crucial to my well-being. Sitting in my darkness is just as necessary as stepping into my light. The key is to find balance, and Mother Nature holds that secret for us. The moon reminds us that it's okay to go through phases. The sun reminds us that we will rise again. The seasons remind us that it's necessary to go through cycles of growth, harvest, death, and rebirth.

"We often forget that we are nature. Nature is not something separate from us. So when we say that we have lost our connection to nature, we've lost our connection to ourselves."
-Andy Goldsworthy

Alongside transforming my mentality, I started transforming my physicality—more specifically, the physical clutter. I had a full house already when Erik moved in; with myself, two kids, a dog, two cats, a boisterous squirrel in my attic (literally *and* figuratively), a closet full of baggage (*also* literally and figuratively), etc. Moving his fully furnished house into mine led to a basement full of duplicates, and an overflow of storage bins. The busy-ness of life and two worlds colliding seemingly so fast meant we procrastinated dealing with the accumulation for too long. We desperately needed to re-organize and downsize. It's taken us over a year, but we've finally reached the measure of minimalism required to move a family of six into a thirty-six-foot bus! Letting go of our attachments to the *materialistic* helped us to continue detaching from the *mentalities* that were holding us back from achieving our desired goals and lifestyle. Finally taking time to unpack the bins, boxes, and baggage was so liberating to our bodies, minds, and souls. A clear space is a clear mind. Not wanting to fall back into our former reality, it has become our goal to collect *fewer things*, and instead collect *more experiences*. Experience fuels growth, which is the direction we are heading for in our tiny home on wheels.

Healing my emotional wounds made me more aware of my overall health and wellness. I took advantage of the accessibility of online courses once again and enrolled in an integrative nutrition course on the brain-gut connection which gave me the awareness needed to regulate my digestive system, which in turn helped me regulate my nervous system! "Irritation in the gastrointestinal system sends signals to the central nervous system that trigger mood changes."[2] *Who knew?!* Staying hydrated, having a healthy sleep routine, practicing mindfulness, Yoga, Reiki, and exploring the natural world around me keeps me in physical, mental, emotional, and spiritual prosperity. Aligning in these realms opened up a door to financial prosperity, as I also used this time to acquire the training and certificates required to lead trauma-informed Hatha Yoga classes and Reiki healing sessions of my own. All of which I can base around my first and most important job title of *Mama*.

> *"We often forget that we are human beings, not human doings."* -Kimberly Hutt

Contrary to what we've always been told to believe, we need time to *do less* and *be more*. Be more present, more aware, more mindful, more creative, more authentic, more connected, and more whole. Managing symptoms allows us to *do more*, but healing ourselves ultimately allows us to *be more*. If you grant yourself the time to deconstruct the layers of yourself that were painted on by others, and reconstruct yourself in alignment with your core beliefs and values, you'll be building your truth on a sturdier foundation—nobody's doubt will ever again be able to crack it. Once I peeled off the layers and rewired my subconscious to work *with* me rather than *against*, I made it back to that creative, spontaneous, dreamer of a girl who got painted over to please others.

Establishing healthy boundaries is a great way to practice self-love. Giving the proper respect to our own physical space, headspace, and authenticity helps us convey our message of what we will and will not tolerate from others. Become so understanding and knowledgeable that you become bulletproof to the situations that used to wound you. Know that the way others interact with you is most likely a projection of their own insecurities and scars. Let their bullets ricochet back to them so their own lessons can recycle until they're ready to heal. Healing the wound requires *feeling* the wound.

Although I don't claim the label of my diagnosis into my current reality, the characteristics associated with it helped me recognize where some of my personality traits were merely mechanisms, stemming from my experiences. When we are living in states of survival from any extent of trauma or cognitive manipulation, our whole reality is distorted, leaving

---

2 Colleen De Bellefonds, "Everything You Need to Know about How Stress Can Impact Your Gut Health," Well+Good, June 9, 2020, https://www.google.com/url?q=https://www.wellandgood.com/stress-gut-health/&sa=D&source=editors&ust=1621646299747000&usg=AOvVaw01jI5yD-pDQfo6pNf6u7t1.

it difficult to imagine any other way to live than the one we know. The beliefs I adopted about myself and the world around me affected my thoughts—and therefore my behaviors and interactions. Rearranging my outlook on life included training my mind to think for itself and healing the wounds that were preventing me from finding my truth.

*"The moment you change your perception is the moment you rewrite the chemistry of your body."
-Dr. Bruce H. Lipton. Now that's spilling some good tea, Lipton.*

The best way to raise children to be their authentic selves is to model for them what it looks like to be shamelessly you. Be patient with yourself as you unlearn the generational trauma unintentionally passed down to you. There is nothing wrong with you. You are not broken. We are here to feel, to adapt, to grow, to share, to love, to be broken down, and to build ourselves back up stronger every time.

*"A woman who heals herself heals her mother, heals her daughter, and heals every woman around her."
-Lisa Hillyer*

Chapter Three

Awakening To Happiness

"Life is way too short to look back and think:
Man, I should have, and I could have."

Pina Crispo

PINA CRISPO

www.ChicMamma.ca

ig: @chic_mamma | fb: @chicmamma
t: @chic_mamma

Not all mamas are created equal, and when it comes to *Chic Mamma*, Pina Crispo, you'll quickly learn just how unique she truly is!

What is *Chic Mamma*? It's the brand Pina solely founded in 2011 to help other mamas with their own unique children and parenting styles.

What makes her a unique mama? She is the ultimate radio chick host and producer of *The Parenting Show* on Global News Radio 640 Toronto (the ONLY parenting show on terrestrial radio in Canada). Pina is also a voice actor and voice coach. But wait! There's more! She also shares her passion and knowledge of radio and branding as a college professor at Humber College in Toronto where she teaches Media Branding and Creative Content Development in their Radio Broadcasting program, and she's an award-winning, best-selling author, too!

Pina has always been one to want it all and do it all, and between the *Chic Mamma* brand and her radio and online personality, Pina truly embodies her brand.

She is an honest, authentic, true-to-life mama (to her kids Samantha, Liliana, and Marcus) with style, humor, and all things in between. She tells it like it is and never holds back, which has been the foundation on which she has built her mama tribe.

Chic Mamma, Pina Crispo . . . she's as real as it gets!

Awakening To Happiness

I was not born to exist; I was born to live! Think about that for a second because, to be honest, it was something I never really paid attention to, something I never really thought about until this past year.

The ball dropped, the clock struck midnight and just like that, 2020 arrived. I was super stoked; I was celebrating what was probably my best career year to date, and I was pumped for what the new year had in store. I can't explain it, but I felt like 2020 was going to bring some major shifts and changes my way, and I was excited! You see, 2019 was a year of reflection. I had many things happen—some small but impactful, and some major—that shifted things for me. During a lot of solo travel that year for work, I found myself thinking and digging deep into things that I had buried for so long. The year peaked on a high note with momentum and drive, and I felt good about what was to come.

Now, was everything perfect in my life? Fuck no! I had parts of my life that were fucking amazing, and others that weren't good at all—but then again, whose life is perfect? The people in the magazines who are photoshopped? The stars in Hollywood who we see on scripted "reality" TV shows? Or maybe it's the content creators and influencers on social media who try to tell you they are "real," yet they perfectly curate and stage each photo and story they post to sell you their false reality? It doesn't exist and never has! At the end of the day, we all have aspects of our lives that are awesome and wonderful, and some that need work, improvement, and growth. Aspects of my life that needed attention for so long were neglected because I couldn't see things clearly and for what they truly were. It was as though I had blinders on—blinders that were finally being removed. Blinders that didn't allow me to see my self-worth, blinders that caused self-doubt, and blinders that were holding me back. So, with this realization, was I excited for the coming year? Hell ya!

It started off with a bang; 2020 was great! My radio show (*The Parenting Show* on Global News Radio 640 Toronto) was doing fantastic, and life as a professor at Humber College was going well. I was working with my business partner, Andrew, on running another one of our voice-over workshops, and my content creator work for *Chic Mamma* was amazing—like so amazing, I had landed a major client who I had been after for a long time. To top it all off, mom-life with the kids was smooth sailing!

That didn't last long, though, because once March hit, everything went to shit. That weird fucked-up virus that was all over the news arrived here in Toronto, and I went from a normal life of being at a Lumineers concert one minute—singing, dancing, and hugging strangers around me—to a life with masks, gloves, sanitizers, and social distancing. I couldn't wrap my head around it. I seriously felt as though I was living a bad dream; it was so bizarre, and with each day that passed, it got worse.

We went from 1 to 100 in a blink of an eye,
and before we knew it, we were in a state of
emergency and were dealing with a worldwide
pandemic; it was scary!

COVID-19 caused us to go into lockdown; schools were closed, people were instructed to work from home, *The Parenting Show* went on hiatus because I wasn't allowed to go into the radio station, and Humber College moved all our classes to online learning because the campus had been shut down. We literally had to stay home unless you were deemed essential—a front-line worker—or you had to pick up groceries or medications (which were pretty much the only stores you could visit).

With the exception of my kids, everything I loved was taken from me, and I started to freak out. I had no radio, no teaching, no voice work, no kickboxing, and what really got me was no family, no friends, and no hugs! It started to take a toll on me—plummeting me from my high to an all-time low. I was doing my best to work from home while trying to homeschool Samantha (eight), Liliana (six), and Marcus (four). It was a disaster; one minute, I would be fine and thinking to myself, *You got this, Pi*, and then the next I would be bawling my eyes out because all I wanted to do was see and hug my mom without having to worry whether there was enough distance between us.

It didn't take much time for the anxiety to kick in. Simple everyday tasks were overwhelming. My motivation and drive went out the window, and I didn't want to do anything. I knew I had to try, and I pushed myself to hold it together because I had three little ones depending on me. The mom-guilt had set in, which went hand in hand with negative self-talk and the feelings of not being good enough or having what it takes to be the mom I needed to be for my kids, to be a successful entrepreneur, a college professor, radio host and producer, all while trying to write my first co-authored book *Mama's Gotta Work!*

I would catch myself daydreaming and thinking about life while going about my daily tasks with the kids and work. Nighttime would roll around and I would sit in my spot on the sofa, sometimes with music and sometimes just alone in the dark, and think some more (until 5 a.m. at times), and then eventually I would make my way up to my room and get a few hours of sleep—only to wake up and do it all over again. There were days that I would open my eyes, and everything would be good for a second, and I was all smiles until I realized and remembered what was going on. There were days that I didn't want to get out of bed, and there were days when I would wake up and question if I was awake or dreaming. Yup, it got to the point where I could not tell what was and wasn't reality; it was like I was in the twilight zone.

Here I was, a mom of three who just celebrated her fortieth birthday in quarantine, and I once again found myself reflecting on life more than ever before. I was questioning and re-evaluating everything. What was in alignment, what wasn't; what was bringing me happiness, what wasn't; what I wanted out of life, and where I was going to draw the line on the things that no longer served me and cut them out. The soul-searching had begun on a deeper level than I had ever experienced before. Even in quarantine, the universe was bringing me things, it was bringing people to me, from old friends resurfacing to new friends coming into my life, and I knew that it was all for a reason. They all played (and continue to play) different roles in my life. It was as though they were sent to me to teach me a lesson, make me realize something that maybe I was missing, and even just put a smile on my face on the days when I thought it was impossible.

My life as a content creator also shifted a bit in the social media world; I started to approach things differently. I always took great pride in ensuring that my *Chic Mamma* brand was authentic, never put-on or fake. What you see is what you get; it has always been like this with me and always will be. I've never been one to sugarcoat shit and paint a bullshit picture for people to look at or try to compare themselves to—contrary to the content creators and influencers I referred to earlier, who claim to be "real" when they're anything but. I started to turn my camera on and share exactly what I was feeling: the anxiety, stress, frustrations, and moments of being low—as well as my highs. I also made a point to use my humor as therapy for others, as well as myself.

Making light of the serious situation we were all living through, and making people smile and laugh made me feel better—because it did the same for me in turn, too.

41

As I mentioned, I was co-writing my first book, *Mama's Gotta Work!*, during this time, and there was a message from my chapter that kept smacking me in my face: we need to be happy in life, love ourselves, and take care of ourselves because if we don't do these things, how can we as mothers be there for our kids and lead by example? It was as if the universe was like, "Wake the fuck up, Pi!" Things started to shift and change. I can't explain it; it was just something I felt within me. Being in lockdown forced me to see that my happiness was at stake. Parts of my life that I thought I was okay with, I wasn't. I was instead just comfortable because it was the thing to do for the sake of others. Years and years of existing, not living my life for myself, and putting others and their happiness before mine was something I didn't want to do anymore. I'd known this for years, but I hadn't acted on it out of fear, guilt, and, more importantly, not knowing my self-worth. It was interesting because my thoughts were now aligning with messages that were finding their way to me through signs like music, people returning to my life, or new people entering my life.

I'll never forget during that time, when my self-worth was top of mind, my phone went off; it was a notification with a link to a song; it was Khalid's *Know Your Worth*. I'd never heard of the song before, so I clicked on the link, and as it started to play, my eyes filled, and the tears began to flow. It was as though the song was speaking directly to me; I knew that it was time to put myself first for once. I was ready to admit to myself that my marriage of almost fourteen years was done, and it had been for many moons. I deserved happiness, and he deserved happiness. No matter which way you looked at it, things were not good; we were not happy, and it wasn't healthy for the kids to be living in that environment. It was something that needed to be done, but I didn't out of fear and the happiness of others. I was paralyzed and wasn't able to move forward. I was scared for the kids and what it would do to them. Would they blame themselves for it? Would it fuck them up? Was I selfish? One thing I knew for sure was that things were beyond repair, and this was the end. I'll never forget discussing the situation with my husband while sitting on the sofa one night. Out of nowhere, in my right ear, I heard my late father say to me, "Coraggio," which is the Italian word for courage. It was then I knew in my heart that I was doing the right thing and that my dad, who had been gone for close to five years, was with me and guiding me.

My dad always used to say to me, "Coraggio,
Pina: have courage, be strong, you got this;" and
as always, he was right.

A new door had opened for me, and as painful and difficult as things were, I was happy. Happy that I was putting myself and my happiness first, that I was making myself a priority, and that by doing this, I was showing my kids what is truly important in life. I was also happy to show them that I, their mom, deserved to be happy—and deserved to live my life, instead of just existing through it. I was growing, and I was working on myself. By no means was it easy then, and it still isn't easy now. I knew I needed to work on myself, so I started back on my spiritual journey with my friend, Franca Abate, from *The Soul's Life*. We began doing regular Reiki sessions together. Meditation, listening to and honoring myself became a daily practice. I redid my Reiki Level 1 and 2 certifications and started practicing the therapy with others. It was time, overdue, but never too late.

You see, being a mom means putting the life of your children before yours: their happiness, well-being, goals, and dreams. We often end up forgetting to focus on all those things for ourselves. Life isn't easy, that's for sure, and like I said in the first book, *Mama's Gotta Work!*, "The curve balls will keep on coming, I know that, but fuck, we're moms, and we'll hit each and every one of them outta the park, even if you're down a strike or two." Here I am at forty-one starting over, and let me tell you, it's scary—it's so fuckin scary—but it feels good, and it's exciting.

I'm done existing, I'm here to live, and you can
bet your ass that is exactly what I'm going to do.

I'm living life on my terms now! I have a lot of life left to live, and I'm going to make every minute of it count. It's my time to be happy, and it's time for Samantha, Liliana, and Marcus to see it. Life is way too short to look back and think, *Man, I should have, and I could have*. Regrets are an ugly thing, and I refuse to live with any.

In the words of Eric Roth, "For what it's worth: it's never too late or, in my case, too early to be whoever you want to be. There's no time limit, stop whenever you want. You can change or stay the same, there are no rules to this thing. We can make the best or the worst of it. I hope you make the best of it. And I hope you see things that startle you. I hope you feel things you never felt before. I hope you meet people with a different point of view. I hope you live a life you're proud of. If you find that you're not, I hope you have the courage to start all over again."

Chapter Four

Reiki Infused Formula

"The only thing you can truly control
is the intention you set for your energy."

Whitney Stout

WHITNEY STOUT

www.Ethical-Energy.com
ig: @EthicalEnergy | fb: @EthicalEnergy

t: @Ethical_Energy | gr: Whitney
yt: Ethical Energy | p: Ethical Energy

Whitney Stout is a Project Doula, Logistical Consultant, Copywriter for *Soulpreneurs*, a Legal Aid Attorney, and an Award-Winning, Best-Selling Author. She is a practitioner of quantum shamanism, certified by the *Contemporary Shamanism Training Institute*, as well as certified in Reiki II. Whitney is the creator of *Ethical Energy*, mother of a human baby, mom to five cats, ISTP spouse of her ESTJ Twin Flame, and resides in Lake City, South Carolina.

Reiki Infused Formula

This really isn't the story I signed up to tell. In the midst of a second-trimester hormone-induced personal-power high, I boldly declared that I was going to have a tale to tell about intentional living, natural pregnancy, and the miracle of breastfeeding. Spoiler alert: my baby is now formula fed, I had a C-section, and my prenatal diet involved Mountain Dew.

When we were sixteen, on our third date, my husband asked me to be the mother of his children. For twelve years, I insisted I did not want children; I didn't allow myself to imagine a future where I was a mother. I had used the Nuva Ring as birth control for years but had stopped using hormonal birth control in an attempt to balance the symptoms of polycystic ovarian syndrome with herbs (raspberry leaf and nettles worked wonders for me, by the way). I began to learn about cyclical embodiment—the idea that the menstrual cycle is a mirror of the seasonal shifts of Mother Earth. Each month, I experienced an inner-spring where I felt optimistic and full of possibility, an inner-summer where I manically started projects, an inner-fall where I looked at the past two weeks and thought, *Oh shoot, dial it back*, and an inner-winter where I questioned everything and wanted to declutter my house and quit my job. As I became more in tune with my inner energetic shifts, the start of my period brought with it a heavy sadness.

I was mourning the lack of a pregnancy I wouldn't allow myself to even try to have.

One night on divinely inspired impulse, my son was conceived on Ostara during a sex magick-based fertility ritual. We chanted along with the song *Othun* by Heilung, called down his spirit, and felt our child's chakra centers map to his new DNA. When I announced my pregnancy, people's instinct was to ask if the pregnancy had been intentional, and if so, would I have still chosen to conceive had I known what was in store for 2020. I imagine their intention was to open a dialogue about how I was doing, but I always felt a subcurrent of judgment in the question. Like it was somehow selfish or ill-thought-out to get pregnant during these uncertain times. But aren't all times uncertain? The COVID-19 virus was an abrupt reminder to humanity that our existing systems and structures were all an illusion. We knew of COVID when we conceived, but rather than serve as a deterrent, the shifting landscape of the pandemic made it seem more imperative than ever before to live, create, and connect with joy.

That joy and divine inspiration we felt during the conception of our child was a fragile thing. I was alone a lot during my pregnancy. My spouse was a mechanic at a canned food factory. He was working twelve to fourteen hours a day, seven days a week as his employer attempted to keep stores stocked. He was so exhausted he could barely stay awake once coming home, much less help around the house or hold space for hormonal meltdowns. My parents were both healthcare workers and couldn't come around. I was classified as an essential worker, and I lived in a state that never implemented a mask mandate and only partially shut down for about two weeks before beginning to reopen. I didn't have the choice to quarantine. The one midwife that served our area was overloaded with homebirth requests and I couldn't get on the list. My only other prenatal care option was the local hospital where I was told all prenatal care was going to be provided in accordance with their internal policy and care schedules, so my options to opt for or refuse certain things were rather non-existent. It was their way or the highway. I wasn't allowed a support person at ultrasound appointments or visits. At the time, the policy was that should I end up testing positive for COVID, I would be put in an isolated COVID room and allowed no support person and would birthe alone with strangers.

> *We embarked on this journey with a dedication to crafting our parenting reality through careful, intentional living, but at every juncture, COVID had taken away my power of choice.*

I became very attached to the idea of salvaging some aspect of my intimate homebirth fantasy and was hell-bent on a natural, unmedicated vaginal delivery. As the pregnancy progressed, my son appeared healthy but remained head up. I melted down about the prospect of a C-section. I spent the next few days in a research frenzy, convinced I could *will* this baby to turn. I read *Spinning Babies*, downloaded a hypnosis track, and researched the procedure that could be done to try and manually turn him.

A friend pointed out to me that my son felt my feelings, lived in my energy field, and of course, knew what was going on with me. She asked me to remember my belief that our souls choose our bodies and parents before we incarnate earthside, so my son chose me as his mother. Beyond that, she asked me to consider the idea that my son had his own ideas about how he wanted to be born. Perhaps my son was choosing a birth that he thought would be in my highest good. Later that night, I tried the breech baby hypnosis track. I was guided to not only connect with my body, but to open a conversation with my baby. A conversation in which I asked him how he was feeling about turning. Through that connection with my unborn child, I was reminded that this child is his own human. On some level, I had been treating this spirit as more like an organ of mine than as his own sovereign being. I opted out of the procedure to try and turn him, never started the exercises, and decided to honor the transmission I felt from his soul.

I was still so very angry. Angry that everywhere around me was fear, divisiveness, and political ideological warfare related to the 2020 presidential election. Angry that the divine initiation of birth was going to instead be a scheduled surgical procedure. Above all else, I was angry that I was angry. Why couldn't I appreciate that he appeared healthy? Why wasn't that enough? My sacral chakra—the center of passion, creativity, and the womb—was poisoned with dark and heavy energies. Energies fed by my fury at the powerlessness I felt to control my pregnancy story. I didn't want to bring this energy to my son's birth.

I truly wanted to bring him into a world where I was sourcing my energy from gratitude and joy.

Although I am a Reiki practitioner and Quantum Shamanism healer-in-training, I felt like I needed to call in support to hold space for me and to clear this self-inflicted energetic emotional womb (or what could also be referred to as getting over my own bullshit). Synchronistically, the practitioner who was available was the same woman who predicted his conception. As we worked to clear the low vibe garbage I had seeded into my soul, I began to release the absurdity of the illusion of control. Surrender is always a concept I have struggled with. Surrender seemed like giving up. But I realized that surrender, the necessary ingredient to living in flow, was really about accepting that the only thing you can truly control is the intention you set for your energy.

After the energetic clearing of the Reiki session, I shifted my focus from trying to manifest certain circumstances to trying to manifest the energy I wanted to bring to the situation. It's funny how the universe provides a training ground for our growth. I never did come to embrace the concept of a scheduled C-section. When the time came to put my intention-setting commitment to the test, I did not have a smooth start.

Once we parked our car in the parking lot, anxiety like I have never experienced before slammed into me. I froze, then sobbed, then as we tried to walk in, I stopped to take breaks to sob some more. I was so damn scared. Scared of surgery, scared the baby wouldn't be okay, scared of just all of it. It was like all the spiritual work I'd done over years had never happened and I was the sentient embodiment of fear.

When we checked in at the hospital, a trainee met me at the desk to review the consent paperwork. The trainee presented one form to me with this explanation, "This is a form saying that if things go south and the worst happens, which is a C-section, you understand that they will do that." Clearly, this trainee had me mixed up with someone who was supposed to be there for a vaginal delivery. I really tried not to be an asshole. But then she presented the next form with the explanation, "This is the form you sign if there is some kind of thing you don't want to happen." I then snapped at this poor woman sarcastically signing the form while commenting, "The only thing I didn't want was a C-section, but obviously my pregnancy has *gone south*."

I was shown to my room, given a hospital gown, and told to strip down and change. I shut myself in the bathroom petulantly, refusing to change my clothes for a good half hour, just not feeling ready to set all these events in motion. Once I put the gown on, I planted myself in a chair, not wanting to get in the hospital bed. Eventually, the time came to turn myself over to the medical-industrial complex. A flurry of activity started as I was hooked up to monitors and IVs. Every time a well-meaning staff member came in to introduce themselves and asked me how I was doing, I snidely quipped, "I'm here because things have gone south and I need a C-section."

It didn't matter how I felt because I didn't have any choices . . . did I?

Around about the fourth time I made a "gone south" reference, my husband leaned in and whispered, "Honey, you've made this a thing, it doesn't have to be a thing. You have to make a choice, is this really the energy you want to bring to this day?" My response was a middle finger. The anesthesiologist then came in. He was a man, and this just pissed me off. I just felt an instant hostility about an unknown man in my birth space. He asked me how I was doing, and I insincerely responded something along the lines of "super-duper fantastic." He took a long look at me, answering, "I think you're being facetious and aren't doing okay at all." I then refused to speak to anyone.

Once in the operating room, it was time for the epidural. They asked me to sit on the edge of the table and "hunch over." Because of my son's positioning, it was nearly impossible to get my spine shaped right. The first attempt didn't work. The second attempt wasn't going well. Three people started giving me instruction at the same time, I began to have a panic attack, and I could overhear a hushed conversation behind me about whether I would need to be put to sleep because I was clearly starting to freak out, and they weren't sure I could handle what was going on.

That same anesthesiologist interrupted that conversation and pointed to most of the room, announcing that their energy was unhelpful and to get out. I was sobbing and apologizing for not being able to follow the instructions, scared I wouldn't get numbed, and so scared the ultimate agency removal would occur: me being unconscious for the birth because I couldn't get control of my energy.

He stopped everything to take a moment with me. He told me that my husband had pulled him aside and explained I had a history with anxiety, and that while I've done well for years now, this day was getting the better of me. He told me that his wife had an anxiety disorder and that he had an entire cart of meds that could make the fear go away if I decided anything going on was too much, but that I would forget meeting my son. He told me I was not failing at anything and that my only job was to look into the eyes of the nurse that remained in the room and pay attention to her touch. The nurse stood in front of me, elbows applying light pressure to my shoulders, palm gently pushing my sternum to help me focus on how to shape my body. She maintained eye contact while getting me to slowly breathe, as we all set the intention to bring me back from that brink of panic. The next thing I knew, I was lying down, my spouse stroking my forehead, basking in the glow of the anesthesiologist and the nurse telling him how brave and strong I had been. My son was born moments later.

Remember earlier in the story how I was all empowered about my bad-ass intuition? I was knocked down a peg by the heightened awareness of mortality brought about by the daily death rates and infection counts. As a parent, living in alignment with my spiritual truth is literally staking my child's life and entire construct of reality on my intuition. It takes an anime character's level of commitment to combat the doubt-gremlins, and it's a daily effort to nurture that quality of self-trust. The fear-based messaging surrounding COVID and the constant bombardment of "Don't you want your child to thrive?" messages that are shoved at pregnant women and new moms had swayed me out of believing that I had the ability to choose to have faith that everything could be okay. I only have the memory of my son's first cries and the tears of joy in my spouse's eyes because two men—two husbands—stepped into the birth space and committed to helping me feel proud of myself and safe.

Now when I question the validity of my intuitive choices, I look at the smiling face of my little baby.

The energy that sourced the decision to bring him into my world cannot steer me wrong. My body nurtured and grew this tiny boy without needing me to instruct it or tell it what to do. I simply had to be, trust, and hope. Going forward, I don't know how gracefully I'm going to handle this motherhood thing. Every day I have to recommit to my desire to create my energetic and emotional reality. But no matter what, I will find a way to show my child that we can live a life sourced from joy, and I will find the faith to believe that spirit will provide us people to support our ascension out of darker days.

Chapter Five

Team Work Makes
The Dream Work!

"I wish I could tell you that I survived all of this because I slept a healthy number of hours each night, I exercised regularly, I ate well, and I didn't drink much . . ."

Leanne Sigrist

LEANNE SIGRIST

www.countrycornerbuns.com
ig: @country.corner.buns | fb: @countrycornerbuns

Leanne is a wife, mother to four young children, and a trained and licensed paralegal. She grew up on a farm in Perth, Ontario, and now lives with her family in Oshawa, Ontario.

She has been with her husband, Bernie, for over thirteen years—and maybe one day she'll write a chapter about how they met. Together they spent six years living in Switzerland, traveling through Europe, and their eldest child was born there. After they returned to Ontario in 2014, they bought her husband's family bakery. They have operated it alongside one another ever since—and they still manage to have a lot of fun and laugh together.

Leanne loves good food, good wine, gardening, and dancing. If you ever ask her, the glass is always half full!

Team Work Makes The Dream Work!

Many small business owners would probably agree that the watchword of the pandemic was "pivot." Before the pandemic, I never used the word in a business sense. To be honest, I'm not sure that word is the most appropriate. I think "survive" is a better fit and more honest. It was, quite honestly, do or die.

On March 13, 2020, my daughter, who is our oldest and was six at the time, got off the bus that afternoon ready to enjoy March break—one whole week off of school! Boy, was that the understatement of 2020. I picked up our four year old son from his Pre-K school, then our youngest two boys from daycare, and we all went home—me knowing that something scary was hovering in the news, and them not having a care in the world!

We tried to start work normally on Monday, March 16, 2020, but by Wednesday my husband and I had to do one of the hardest things we've ever done as small business owners: we had to let our staff of twenty know that the jobs they'd worked at so loyally for years, had vanished (temporarily), almost overnight. It was a truly awful day. We went home with the weight of the world on our shoulders, not having a clue where the world, or our business, was heading. The wine didn't taste good that night, but we drank it anyway; we lost the cork.

We had been operating a wholesale bakery that we bought from my husband Bernie's family six years prior. The business had been in his family for over thirty years.

We were glued to the news for the first couple of weeks, with children running wild and screaming around us, while we tried to wrap our heads around what was happening and how long we thought it might last. We had expected it to last six months.

Once Prime Minister Justin Trudeau announced the nation-wide lockdown, I turned the news off and have rarely watched since. Bernie reads enough news for both of us, and he tells me what I need to know. At this point, there were no financial relief plans in place from our governments, and we had no choice but to figure out a way to keep our livelihood.

We live on a country corner in North Oshawa, Ontario, and our daughter always wanted to sell things on the corner to cottage-goers in the summer months. Cinnamon buns were one of our favorite products from the bakery and they were always number one on our list to sell on the corner one day.

We never thought our backs would be up against the wall one day, leaving us no choice but to make that "one day" today.

Bernie went to work every day after March 18 and did a lot of trial and error, baking dozens of cinnamon buns, shopping for packaging, and contacting printers to get new labels made. Because we operate a wholesale bakery, packaging with labels, etc. was all very new to us. Meanwhile, I was at home caring for (and entertaining) four young children, while constantly brainstorming ways we could survive this pandemic. By March 23, I launched our Instagram and Facebook pages, opened a new email account, and *Country Corner Buns* was born.

By March 26, 2020 we were delivering our first order of buns—we were excited but very nervous. We had no clue if it was going to work, or if people would like them. Bernie was up early baking and packing all of the orders. He then came home to get me, and with all four kids in tow (Stanley, our youngest, was only six months old), we loaded up to make twenty deliveries. It felt like the longest delivery trip ever. We underestimated our delivery time by what felt like hours. We pulled over after a few hours when it was getting dark to get our kids dinner—Timbits and chocolate milk for the older three, breast milk for the babe. We weren't sure it was going to be worth it after that. By the end of it I was crying, the kids were crying, Bernie was yelling, and I'm sure I was yelling, too.

I should also tell you, our first orders were supposed to be delivered the day before this, but Bernie is a bit of a perfectionist (which is a great quality to have, don't get me wrong), and he wasn't happy with the cinnamon buns and the way they rose, so the WHOLE production went into the garbage. I cried, Bernie was so mad and frustrated that I couldn't even talk to him about it, and I had to contact every new customer to let them know we were experiencing delays and their orders weren't coming on time. To say we were feeling a bit defeated before we really got started, would be an understatement.

That first day when baking went sideways, Bernie came home, we loaded the kids into the car, and we headed for a playground. The parks were still open at the time, and despite the stress we were both feeling, we did everything we could to not let it affect the kids. We sat on a park bench with Stanley in his stroller, while the other three ran off and played; we each had a beer and tried to forget about what had just happened.

Between working, we hit up as many playgrounds as we could in the first few weeks; it was an escape for us and for the kids. We all loved it;

it was a short period of time where we could put our phones away and forget about reality. Then they closed all of the parks, so Bernie (aka our version of MacGyver) built one in our backyard, and the kids barely used it! It was an escape for Bernie to come home and work on, however, and the kids loved being part of the building process with him.

Let's get back to the buns. After our first delivery, word started to spread. We witnessed the power of social media like never before. People were posting pictures and reviews, and they were loving them. This was a source of comfort and joy during a time of panic and despair. We were shocked and thrilled—and terrified. We had no idea where this was going to go, but we were running with it. We had no choice.

We had the best supporters we could have asked for. Every friend, neighbor, or acquaintance who knew us in the Durham Region either ordered to try them, or they sent them to someone in our area, or shared it on their social media if they lived too far away. We also became part of the small business community in Durham, and that has been one of the most fulfilling parts of this experience for me.

We'll never forget the support and kindness we felt from our friends, family, and many strangers during those first few months. It was incredible.

I was taking orders by Facebook messenger, Instagram messenger, and email. For the first week or two it was busy, but manageable, and then things really started to take off. I was receiving messages by the hour all day long, so many of them that it was taking me more than a day to respond to many of them. My phone, literally, never stopped dinging with new messages. I was so busy with the kids during the day that I couldn't read any messages until they were in bed—I was also so worried I'd miss orders if I did something and forgot later on—and that stressed me out hard some days. I had to turn the ringer on my phone off. I was anxious to stay on top of the orders and the work, but I was also very aware that I needed to be *Mom* too.

Let me paint a real picture for you before I go any further. During these first weeks of starting, Bernie was waking up and going to work to bake between 2:00-3:00 a.m. each day. I would wake up with the kids and feed them cinnamon buns (quality control was important), then I'd finalize the delivery routes on an excel sheet, and I would head out to start deliveries around noon—as soon as Bernie walked in the door. I would put "real" clothes on and clean myself up minutes before Bernie arrived home. Most days I would take Stanley with me because he was still really young and I was breastfeeding, and he had barely started solid food. Also, leaving

Bernie with four kids (one of which needed to be bottle fed), after he'd barely slept, wasn't fair—and I was trying to keep a good balance.

Stanley and I would deliver for three to five hours each afternoon. I would feed him right before we left and cross my fingers that I could finish as many deliveries as possible before I had to pull over, climb into the back to feed him again, and strategically change his diaper on the seat of the van. Where are my travelling moms at? You know the drill! After four kids, I could change a diaper on a bicycle seat if I had to. It's hard to remember now, and I'm sure he had his moments where he cried, but overall, he was a real champ.

I would get home from delivering, Bernie would have cooked dinner, we'd eat, and Bernie and the kids would go to bed. I would stay up until 2 a.m. answering messages and processing orders; all of which were done manually. There were many nights where Bernie would be coming down to head to work, and I'd turn the coffee on for him as I was headed up to bed. Dream team.

It got to the point where we both had to start delivering, which meant all four kids were coming along too, and neither of us were sleeping very much. At first, the kids were excited, but they soon got bored when they realized they couldn't get out of the vehicle and help deliver because we all had to be careful of "germs"—and mom and dad had to wear gloves and masks when they delivered. Eventually it got to the point where once they heard the words "we have to deliver," it was nothing but groaning and whining from all of them.

Fast forward to Christmas 2020—it was the first real break we took since March. We were SO mentally, emotionally, and physically exhausted. But we were also SO happy to have the holidays upon us and nothing but time to relax at home and be with the kids. For some people who have barely left their house since March, this must sound crazy, but we were not in that boat—I'm not sure any small business owner was. It felt like we hadn't come up for air until now.

During a typical December, pre-pandemic, my husband worked sixteen hour days, seven days a week, from the end of November through to December 24. It felt like we never got excited for Christmas until the 24th, and then it was madness to prepare when all we wanted to do was sleep.

We were so grateful to still be busy this past December, but it was a different busy for us, a much more fulfilling and controlled one—and a MUCH healthier one. Although we weren't able to celebrate the holidays with our extended families, it was one of the best Christmas holidays we've ever had with our family.

I wish I could tell you that I survived all of this because I slept a healthy amount of hours each night, I exercised regularly, I ate well, and I didn't drink much . . .

All of that is so far from the actual truth. I've lost so much sleep, I'm dying to exercise regularly, but find every excuse there is not to. I ate two cinnamon buns and had two coffees for breakfast every day for months, and I had at least one drink a day for longer than I'd like to admit—just to cope with stress and the madness that was going on around us in the world.

But I'm here, still not at the end of it, but still pushing through. Some days I thrive, some I barely survive. Although it may not be going in all of the ways that I want it to, I know that I'm the only one that can change a lot of that. With spring on the horizon, I'll get back to exercising and eating better, and I know it will make me feel better—but like many things, it's easier said than done sometimes—especially while trying to survive a pandemic as a small business family, with four small children, a Saint Bernard, two cats, and a home to maintain.

Us moms have to cut ourselves some slack. We do all of the things, all of the time and I'll be the first to admit that I don't make myself a priority—and sometimes I think my kids and husband suffer the brunt of that. As busy as we all are, we *need* to take time for ourselves. It's been said many times before and I'll say it again, you can't take care of others if you're not taking care of yourself. This couldn't be truer for a mom, even if it means staying up way too late to watch trashy shows because that's the only quiet time you've had all day. Guilty as charged!

Please don't think for a second that we live this perfect little life, because we don't. We're very normal. We yell, we overreact, and we (I) cry, but we move on from it. The storm passes, we forgive, we forget, we dish out a lot of hugs, we learn from our mistakes and, most importantly, we laugh. Laughter is truly one of the best medicines, and lucky for me—and anyone else who has the pleasure of knowing him—I married one of the funniest guys out there and he's forever making us laugh.

Moms don't always deserve all of the credit, especially not in this case. My husband is the pillar of strength in this family and the glue that holds us together. He works tirelessly for our family, and he and I are very much a team in everything that we do. When doing things as a family, often one of the six of us will randomly yell, "teamwork" and the rest of the gang will respond, "makes the dream work!" It makes me smile every time.

My family truly is a dream team. My husband didn't think for one second about giving up, and my kids are amazing for being so strong, resilient, and loving throughout. What I hope for them is that they learn to never give up and that this is the only global pandemic they'll face in their lifetime.

We work hard, we play hard, and most of all, we love hard.

Section Two

Adapting To Change:
Adjusting The Sails

"Motherhood changes everything."

~ Adriana Trigiani

FEATURING:

Elizabeth Meekes
Candace Clark Trinchieri
Krysta Lee
Emanuela Martina Hall
Jaime Hayes & Marnie VandenBroek-Hookey

The Un-Becoming

"True strength is soaking in all of our humanness.
It's being at home with who we truly are. It's being
vulnerable and compassionate; holding yourself;
wrapping her in a blanket of love; allowing her the
safety to be exactly as she needs to be in each
moment, free from who she thinks she should be."

Elizabeth Meekes

ELIZABETH MEEKES

www.elizabethmeekes.com
ig: @lizmeekes | fb: @lizmeekes

Elizabeth Meekes is a Consciousness Coach, holistic practitioner, numerologist, writer, speaker, and podcaster. After graduating from Wilfrid Laurier University, her love for learning soon led her to training to become a Holistic Practitioner and then a certified Life Coach through the Centre for Applied Neuroscience. She has since upgraded her training and qualifications with certifications as a Numerologist and Consciousness Creator with her mentor, Harriette Jackson.

Elizabeth does life with her partner Steve and their two boys, Rowan and Arion. She is a truth seeker and a change maker. She is here for growth, connecting with Mother Nature, moving slow, and breathing deep. She is on a mission to stand raw and true in her power, to face her shadows and do the work to heal, to keep standing back up every time she falls, and to hold and create space for you to do the same. Elizabeth is passionate about holding space for creativity and growth and allowing our children the space to soak in their own creative genius. Using a holistic approach that focuses on root-cause solutions and deep healing, she guides people to develop a greater understanding of self, to meet their shadows, and to peel back the layers of expectations in order to come home to their truest selves. She's here to create real change, to burn down the patriarchy, and to raise conscious children.

The Un-Becoming

When I was seventeen, I lost one of my closest friends to cancer. After fighting with everything he had, he passed three weeks before his nineteenth birthday. I couldn't allow myself to feel the level of grief that was present for me. So I did what I knew best, I pushed that shit down deep, and I flashed my perceived strength to the world. I say perceived strength because in those moments, in that time in my life, I truly believed it was strength I was demonstrating. Now I am much more familiar with the embodiment of true strength, and it could not be farther from what I displayed back then.

My seventeen-year-old self believed it was more important to show the world how "well" I could move through hard things, than to actually feel the hard things. It was so surface-level, the way I showed up for myself, what I believed to be strength, to be growth. I remember conversations with my friends about how much shit we had been through and how strong we were to have gotten through it. Except, we hadn't actually moved through any of it; at least, I certainly had not. I was holding it so deeply in my cells and in my tissues, refusing to allow myself the expression and release of what was truly present, beneath all of that perceived strength.

I want you to know that as I share this, I am holding so much space for that younger version of myself. I am wrapping her in all of my love and compassion and grace. I hold no judgment or resentment for the armor she carried, it was all she knew. She was doing the best she could with all that she had. I love her so fucking much for all that she is, because she is me and I am her. Without being in that space, where it seemed the only option was to suit up in armor so shiny that it hid away all of the pain I didn't want to move through, without all of those experiences, I would not be in the space I am now.

The difference between then and now is acceptance and honoring all that I am, this feeling of home that resides within my whole being, my light and my dark. At seventeen, I was not willing to meet my shadows, and unless I could bring myself to meet them—and accept them—I could not honor all of me. In that time, I was living as a fragment of my whole being.

THE SHADOW SELF

The shadow self encompasses everything outside of your consciousness, all of the aspects that we avoid accepting in ourselves. We tend to view these aspects as negative, thus we tuck them deep into the dark of the shadow self. So, you may think: *well of course I don't feel like hanging with my shadow self, she's all kinds of fucked up.* I hear you, I've been there, hence the armor for so many years. But here's the problem: an unwillingness to meet the shadow self prevents us from growth and has us in a state of by-passing.

> *"One does not become enlightened by imagining figures of light, but by making the darkness conscious."[1]*
> *-Carl Jung*

This gets even more problematic because the state of by-passing has us sit in a whole stew of toxic positivity.

TOXIC POSITIVITY IN MOTHERHOOD

Why as mothers do we feel so much pressure to love every minute of our lives? To slap a smile on and push all our icky feelings down so deep that no one can see our humanness? Heaven forbid you have an icky emotion, or a shitty day, or parenting feels really hard; all of a sudden you are the worst mom to have ever existed. Or we create that story for ourselves because of all the shit we see around us creating the expectations of how it *should* be. All of the expectations of motherhood—the "shoulds" that are pushed on us from literally every direction—leave us feeling like shit because meeting every one isn't realistic. We make ourselves wrong if we struggle.

Let's take a look at social media as one example. Although more and more women are showing up in their truth and their humanness in the realm of social media, the vast majority remain a perfectly curated highlight reel. What this creates is the façade, the illusion that the perfection we are seeing is reality. This is so troubling because the standard of perfection within life and motherhood that is portrayed is unattainable and fake. It does not display the true vastness of our humanness, and it

---

1 Carl Jung, *The Collected Works of CG Jung, Volume 13: Alchemical Studies,* ed. Gerhard Adler and R.F.C. Hull, *Princeton University Press* (Princeton University Press, 1967), 264.

completely dismisses the experiences of so many. When we consume too much of this curated content, we often judge and blame ourselves for moments where we are purely human, forgetting that the point of being human has absolutely nothing to do with perfection. Harriette Jackson teaches that the first incarnation's intention is to have a human, physical, and emotional experience. This includes all the emotions, my friends, even the ones we don't love.

The way this translated for me was it reaffirmed my first instinct when I was struggling: to pick up my armor and flash my shiny perceived strength so that people couldn't see me, so that they couldn't find out how human I really am.

Now, as a mother, all of that grief and sadness and anger that was held so tightly in my tissues began to bubble to the surface and manifested as intense anxiety. I had a brand-new baby, and I was so filled with fear that the worst possible thing would happen to him or to my partner, leaving him without his dad. This came as panic attacks in the night. I would hold my new baby and lay my hand on my husband to remind myself they were both breathing. Yet, I felt like I couldn't. *I could not breathe*. For so many nights, I sat there crying, struggling to catch my breath, moving through everything as if I had lost them, unable to calm myself with the reality of their breath under my hands. At night I could not breathe, and then as soon as morning came, I picked up my armor and refused to show anyone I was struggling. I didn't even tell my husband. I was so ashamed. I believed this anxiety meant there was something wrong with me because all I could see around me was this insanely unrealistic expectation of the perfect mother. This shame, the refusal to actually be with what was present for me, perpetuated the cycle. Once again, I was faced with emotions that felt too big for me, and I felt wrong for feeling them, or unsure of how to even begin feeling what was present.

My first reaction when I am triggered or avoiding discomfort is to reach for the armor like my younger self; it's the programming my body goes to because I lived inside of it for so long. So, I had to work to become conscious and aware before the armor was on, to heal and reprogram. It was a conscious effort to start meeting my shadows and showing up for myself on a much deeper level. I had to learn all of this real quick when I became a mom. Children are great mirrors. They trigger the shit out of us and show us all the stuff we tried to tuck away. In these moments of trigger, until we become aware and can approach it consciously, we will find ourselves very quickly going to our programmed trauma response.

I took a break from writing this in the notes on my phone to scroll Instagram. When I opened the app, the first thing I read was a quote by

Toni Jones:

> *"Trauma teaches you to close your heart and armor up. Healing teaches you to open your heart and boundary up."*[2]

This is what I'm speaking about. I was living in a trauma response, keeping myself safe in the only way I knew how, with all of my armor. Except now, I was playing out this pattern with my family. I was closing myself off from so much around me. I realized how unsustainable it was. It was no longer just about me. I had to think about the space I wanted to hold for my children. I want them to know and love themselves in all of their beauty, in all of their humanness. I want them to have the tools to hold themselves in their healing and their growth so that they can create a beautiful life on their terms and contribute to the healing of the collective. So that is exactly what I need to do for myself. That's when I started doing the deep, deep work to heal, when I realized it's not just about me, and it's not even just for my children. Yes, it is absolutely for me and for my children, and also for the collective. I'm here for depth, curiosity, truth, and growth; for knowing myself at the core; for understanding my shadows, the old patterns, and narratives; for shedding all of the surface shit until I am the truest expression of me, of my soul, and my humanness, so that I can contribute to the collective healing.

Sounds easy enough, right? Just drop the armor, heal the things, love your life, and contribute to the rising and healing of the collective. I'm sorry friends, there is nothing easy about it. This work is hard, it's deep, dark, and gritty, and it's worth it.

WHERE DO I BEGIN?

I will share with you what worked for me.

I had to take a holistic approach to my mind, body, and soul. I could no longer live with my body disconnected from my mind, and the two were not even in the same book as my soul, let alone on the same page. This meant I needed to get real clear on the connection between my body and my mind. I needed to understand: the way I treat and nourish

---

2 Toni Jones (@iamtonijones), "Trauma teaches you to close your heart and armor up. Healing teaches you to open your heart and boundary up.", Instagram post, February 17, 2021 https://www.instagram.com/p/CLapSKfFGr5/?utm_medium=share_sheet

my body is directly related to the chaos swirling in my mind. And while I was living in that chaos, I had no chance of connecting to my soul.

At this point I was studying to become a holistic practitioner. Talk about perfect timing. The holistic health I focus on has its foundation in root-cause solutions. We are not looking to mask symptoms, but rather get to the root of where they come from, treating the body as the incredibly beautiful, powerful system that it is. This is the approach I will forever take in my own healing, in the work I do with my clients, and in the way I contribute to the collective.

> *I am not interested in surface-level Band-Aids. I am here for root-cause solutions, for getting to the core.*

For us as humans, our root chakra is connected to our first energy body, our Soul body. This is where we need to get back to, where we need to come home to. It all begins with the relationship and depth of understanding we hold with our own self. True strength is soaking in all of our humanness. It's being at home with who we truly are. It's being vulnerable and compassionate; holding yourself; wrapping her in a blanket of love; allowing her the safety to be exactly as she needs to be in each moment, free from who she thinks she *should* be.

As you come home to your Soul, there will be layers that are wildly uncomfortable. So enter into this journey with support. You do not have to do this alone. Allow yourself to create a community of care that holds you, and acts as your mirror for those things that you would rather not see.

This is important to take note of: we are living in entire systems built on the foundation of white supremacy. That means this requires you to take a serious look at where in your tissues you are storing patriarchal conditioning that is rooted deeply in white supremacy, and then take conscious action to dismantle those systems and purge them from your tissues.Rachel Ricketts writes in her book, *Do Better*:

> *"I believe we are all limitless souls having a humxn experience and we all came to Earth at this exact time to learn, unlearn, and, ultimately, heal—ourselves and each other. I believe in the possibility for us to drop the old white supremacist scripts that have been*

holding us back and disconnecting us from ourselves and one another."[3]

The growth for me was and still is, healing from the idea that I need to be anything other than who I am. It is not adding any more armor, but rather slowly slipping out of the armor I knew for so long and continuing to peel back the layers of narratives and expectations, un-becoming everything I thought I needed to be. I say *still is*, because we are never done. Again, this is part of our humanness, that shit all coming back to us when we least expect it. Old habits like reaching for the armor when I thought I had thrown it in the trash for good. Growth is an upward spiral. So, each time you come back to what seems like the same thing, you are one level up. There is new depth each time, new understanding, a new meeting of self. Again, and again, and again, as we move up our spiral. This past year living through the beginning of COVID-19 and all that was 2020, I had to really remind myself to keep doing that inner work. To strip away the armor rather than pile it on. To continue to peel back the layers, meeting new shadows with compassion and grace . . . the un-becoming.

Years ago, when I considered growth, it was all about *becoming*: layering on titles and ideals, ways I could show the world how well I was doing, how shiny my armor was, all that surface-level shit. For me now, growth is meeting my shadows. It's about radical personal responsibility. It's dancing the line between my light and my dark and holding space for my own healing. It's forgiving myself, again and again, allowing grace for the moments that I hadn't yet healed, and for those that are yet to be healed; those moments that still trigger the fuck out of me as I create more space for deeper healing and transformation. It has nothing to do with what's on the surface and everything to do with my inner work. It's the journey; coming home, shedding that which is no longer serving, allowing space for expansion, then doing it all over again, and going a little deeper. Meeting myself again and again. It's the un-becoming.

---

3 Rachel Ricketts, *Do Better - Spiritual Activism for Fighting and Healing from White Supremacy.* (Atria Books, 2021), xvii.

Chapter Seven

Dismantling The Myth of Being The Perfect Mother

"No one else gets to define 'motherhood' for you. There is no one way, there is no right way, and there is certainly no perfect way to be a good mother. It is not about being perfect. The ultimate goal, our only goal, should be to have happy, secure, well-adjusted kids. That only comes from a happy, secure, well-adjusted parent; and sometimes happiness can look a little messy."

Candace Clark Trinchieri

CANDACE CLARK TRINCHIERI

www.infertilitystory.com
ig: @infertilitystories

Candace is a proud mom, an adoption and infertility advocate, writer, and a passionate believer in uplifting and supporting all women as we strive to navigate the landscape of motherhood. The majority of her working life has been spent in fundraising and special events for nonprofits such as Big Brothers Big Sisters, The Alzheimer's Association, RESOLVE, and the Cancer Support Community. From her perspective as a woman of color, she is absolutely thrilled to share her experience, humor, and hard-won wisdom, all from the pandemic-created, makeshift office on her kitchen table. With an ever-present cup of coffee, she enthusiastically tries (and fails) to be the modern-day, do it all, perfect, fix everything, wonder-woman. She makes her chaotic and happy home in Los Angeles with her husband, and seven-year-old son.

Dismantling The Myth of Being The Perfect Mother

All I wanted was to be a perfect mom. So, right from the start, I was doomed to fail. It is hard to live up to your image of perfection. Instead of being perfect, motherhood left me feeling anxious, confused, overworked, and in over my head. I had fought a long, hard battle through infertility and was thrust into motherhood by the adoption of my son.

The adoption process gave me a lot of time to think, prepare, and agonize about what kind of mother I wanted to be, so the picture in my head was crystal clear. I would be organized, ready, warm, loving, and fun. I walked around making a lot of comments about how I was going to seamlessly fold my child into my existing life. I actually believed that being prepared was as easy as reading all the right books, setting up the nursery, and buying up every single baby item that was suggested on the motherhood blogs.

All of this, I believed, was the road map that would lead me to be the perfect parent.

Immediately after my son was born and we brought him home from the hospital, I spent a lot of time pretending—pretending I wasn't tired, that I knew what the hell I was doing, that I wasn't completely overwhelmed, sad, depressed, lonely, and even bored sometimes home alone with my newborn, yearning for adult conversation. Trying to make everything perfect left no room for me to be patient with myself.

Before I became a mom, I heard about something called the "mommy wars." This supposed competition between mothers, where we are pitted against one another and sit in judgment of each other's choices. I made my choices early on and held them up in front of me like a shield before going into an imaginary battle. However, I found there is no mommy war, real or imaginary, between moms who leave the house to go back to work in an office and moms who stay in the home to raise their kids. The reason I think this war doesn't exist is because it is an illusion that women have choices neatly laid out in front of us.

I have learned that the majority of women base their parenting decisions on economic factors and social privilege.

We are bound by our own particular circumstances. Yet, women are often led to believe that there is an unyielding binary choice we must make that decides how much we love our kids. Do we stay home, or do we return to work outside the home? Usually, this decision is completely out of our hands. I remember, in the midst of struggling to decide whether to go back to work, I asked my friend how she came to her decision to return to work immediately after her very short maternity leave. Without missing a beat, she simply replied, "My husband said if I didn't go back to work we would lose the house." In the end, like other women have throughout history, we make the hard and sometimes painful choices that make sense for our families.

There is no one-size-fits-all motherhood. It's okay if you wing it until you find what works—I know that now. They don't give out awards for motherhood, but boy was I killing myself to come in first place. I was, after all, from the generation of women who were told for the first time in history that we were the generation that really could have it all. I could bring home the bacon and fry it up in a pan.

I am woman, hear me roar. Career and family, it was all mine for the taking.

Admittedly, my view of motherhood was skewed. Adopting Max when I was forty-three made me a Generation X mom raising my child amongst Millennial moms. Most, if not all, of my college friends are empty nesters with kids in college. There is even a grandmother or two among my crew while I parent a seven-year-old. As a child of the 1970s, I grew up in a whole different world. It was lax on safety regulations, parental oversight, and strong on independence. Seventies kids were often free-range, latchkey kids. We roamed our neighborhoods, played outdoors by ourselves, walked to the park with our friends, and made our own play-dates with whatever kid was home. My mother, home from a long day at work, served up McDonald's. I played on sports teams where you did not get a trophy for participation.

My childhood was glorious and free, yet I was determined that I would parent in a completely different way. I see the way my mom looks at me. She sees her yoga-loving, healthy-eating, super-careful, helicopter-parent daughter struggle to parent perfectly in this modern age, with a mix of amusement and confusion. She just didn't worry about all the things I worry about.

I learned the hard lesson as a mom, if perfection is your only goal, you will always come up short.

The mom I thought I was going to be, the mom I stressed myself out to be in the first few years of my son's life, and the mom that I was informed that I had to be, would be shocked, dismayed, and smugly superior to the mom that I am now. I now happily find myself a living embodiment of the chaos theory—out of disarray, I have found my perfect order.

Let's be real. There is NOTHING positive about a worldwide pandemic. It completely disrupted life as we knew it and reshaped the way we live, work, and interact with those around us. When my life was turned upside down because of COVID-19, I saw clearly for the first time that there were four myths that I had fallen into believing. These were the myths I had to work through to fully find my happy.

MYTH 1: IT IS EASY TO HAVE IT ALL.

No one has it all, no matter what it looks like on social media. I know that it sounds logical, but this was a hard one for me to stop buying into. The work and home life balance can feel like a never-ending juggle. One thing will always be jumping on top of the other.

When I was staying at home, all I wanted to do was get back to my office. When I was in my office, either I was feeling the guilt of how much I actually loved being at work, twisted up over how much I missed being at home, or jealous of the nanny. I just couldn't find the balance that I had always heard existed. I was drowning trying to "have it all."

Being a mom is all work, whether we get paid for that work or not.

Everyone is going through some type of struggle. Struggle just looks different from person to person and family to family. We all have experienced the crappy days, the crappy weeks; hell, I have even had a crappy year. I realized that having it all was something that was fluid and would change every day because my priorities changed every day. Some days success was as simple as getting out of bed.

MYTH 2: THERE IS A SPECIFIC DEFINITION OF MOTHERHOOD AND HOW IT IS SUPPOSED TO BE.

The expectation that motherhood should come naturally is too much pressure for anyone. There can be a very narrow definition of motherhood and what makes a good mother. It is very often heteronormative, and racially it tends to look very white in images, movies, magazines, and other media. Type in "mom" or "mommy" in a Google search and take a look at what images appear. If I ever smiled that hard my face would hurt.

The danger in presenting a sterile and curated version of motherhood and parenting is that what you see is what you begin to internalize and believe. All families are different, all moms are different, but nothing, no book, no article, and no pre-baby class prepared me in any true way for just how hard it was all going to be.

Not only was the first year rough for me, the first three months of no sleep almost broke me. I didn't think that I could tell anyone how miserable I felt. Of course, the feelings and the phase passed. Max started sleeping through the night, and I was able to get some rest.

Always keep in mind that motherhood is all transitional.

The worst times, they pass, and you all move onto the next thing. And now, at baby showers, when others are laughing sweetly about what is to come, I tell the truth. I tell the expectant mom: "At some point, there is going to be a part of this that is going to be horrible, and you will be frustrated and maybe angry at how difficult it seems. It's okay, it will pass. It will get better, it is all transitional."

MYTH 3: MOTHERHOOD SHOULD TRUMP OVER EVERY ASPECT OF YOUR LIFE.

I hate that I even have to say this, but it is an easy myth to buy into and one of the hardest to reject. Despite everything you may have spent your life believing, motherhood is one aspect of who you are; it is not all you are. You are not selfish for wanting things or time for yourself. You honor your kids and family by not losing who you are. Having a child, becoming a parent is life-changing in all the best ways, but it does not and should not erase that you are a fully actualized, smart, beautiful, sexy, complex, amazing human.

I became a better parent by learning to love and forgive myself.

I became a stronger parent by learning to parent according to what works best for my family, instead of trying to fit into a mold. Losing sight of who you are in pursuit of being a perfect mom will not make anyone happy. Your family needs you to show up, not an altered version of you. Just you, perfectly imperfect. Your kids need to see you lose your temper, get frustrated, argue with your partner. They need to see how you work through and manage your frustration in a positive way. They need to see you being able to disagree and lovingly come together as an example of resolving conflict. Your family needs (and loves) you, in all your glory—not the person that is just a one-dimensional mom. Your family needs the total, incredible woman that you are in real life.

MYTH 4: JUDGING OTHER MOTHERS WILL MAKE MY LIFE BETTER AND CEMENT MY OWN SUPERIORITY.

CAN WE ALL AGREE TO STOP MOM SHAMING! I am not going to pretend that I am not guilty of this in some way. Social media makes mom shaming oh-so-convenient these days. When I think of pictures or posts that have gone viral, I also think of how I would feel if a single moment in my day was blown up on the internet and judged for all the world to see. My mom never had to worry about people pulling out cellphones and blowing her up on YouTube or Facebook.

As mothers, with the deeply personal choices we make regarding raising our kids, our fight is not with one another.

I said before that the mommy wars are fictional. We, as mothers, all want the same thing: happy, well-adjusted kids. We may get to that end in different ways with different philosophies, but we all desire the exact same outcome. There are very different ways of doing things; there does not have to be an absolute right or wrong.

Today, I am on my perch at the kitchen island. I get a bird's eye view to survey not only the mess in my kitchen but also the shambles of my living room. I had cleaned both up last night before going to bed, a futile effort as I can see that my son has decided it was a personal challenge to destroy it in the shortest amount of time. For reasons known only to himself, he has also decided to run around without his pants on and, in full underwear glory, sing a song about farts as he dances around the living room. Intermittently, he will stop his dance and exclaim at the top of his lungs that he does not want to go to school, he has a stomachache, he wants a KitKat, his ankle hurts, and then, just like that, he is distracted by a commercial on TV for one of the few toys he does not yet have. He declares that this is now the only thing in the world that will make him happy, and he needs it right now—today; and then, with the commercial over, he begins the second verse of his fart song.

I sit at the counter and gaze down at the bright red mug in my hands that I received last Mother's Day from my husband and son. It is inscribed with the words "Super Mom, Super Wife, Super Tired". It is chipped in one corner, stained and dirty, half-full of the morning's coffee that has been reheated three times since 7:00 a.m., and it is just now past noon. The morning has been so chaotic that I haven't had time to check my emails or do any work.

Since the COVID-19 pandemic, my husband gets to stay tucked away in his home office, far from the noise and effort of child-rearing, probably enjoying child-free Zoom work meetings and uninterrupted conference calls. I don't let the envy of this new situation turn into the resentment I used to feel. It is what it is, unfair, but now a way of life that I have to navigate. He will pick up the slack and put in his time another way. Maybe I will spend the next Saturday morning in bed alone with a cup of hot coffee and watching reality TV as he takes care of Max and I take care of myself.

Remember, sometimes, it is perfectly okay to make choices that are all about you.

In the past, I would have hated a morning like this one. I would have been stressed because of the disorder and impatiently trying to control it all. Now, I just smile at how happy my kid is in the moment. I relax into the fact that it is all okay. I am doing everything right. I take a sip of cold coffee with the fart song beginning to stick in my head like an old favorite tune. You know what? I am happy. So far, it is a perfect day!

Chapter Eight

What To *Not* Expect, When You're *Not* Expecting

" [Ctrl] Expectations;

[Alt] Attachments;

[Del] Disappointments;

[=] Love Unconditionally."

Krysta Lee

KRYSTA LEE

www.krystalee.com
ig: @krystalee111 | fb: @Krysta.lee.fanpage
li: Krysta Lee | tw: @krysta_lee
yt: Krysta Lee | gr: Krysta Lee

Krysta Lee is an award-winning, best-selling author (*Mama's Gotta Work!*; *Women Let's Rise*), life coach, actor, and singer with over three decades of combined professional experience. She is featured in magazines and online publications; has appeared on numerous TV shows, films, radio and podcast productions; performs live on stage, speaks at special events, and is regularly interviewed as a special guest across various media platforms.

While pursuing her goals and actively helping people transform from wanderers to *Warriors*, Krysta Lee uses her voice as an activist for personal growth. She's an optimist, a goal-getter, and a big dreamer with a deep love for the arts. Empowering others is important to her, and she's on a mission to inspire as many people as possible to dig deep and level-up their lives, too!

Krysta Lee resides in Prince Edward County, Ontario, Canada, with her partner-in-shine, DJ, their two starseed children, Jaxon and Lillee, and a beautiful menagerie of faminals.

What To *Not* Expect, When You're *Not* Expecting

Full disclosure: while writing this chapter, I felt called to *go there*, so let this be a trigger warning for sensitive content. As taboo as some of the following topics may be, I'm speaking from my own personal experience and can only share what I know as my truth. The intention for this piece is an eye-opening and inspiring one that's filled with unconditional love, light, and lessons. Please take from these pages only that which resonates with you, dear Mama.

This is the accumulation of a fraction of the conscious growth I've experienced in my journey throughout motherhood thus far. It would be next to impossible to document everything into one chapter (plus, what mom with two-under-four has *that* kind of time?!). So, I've selected some of my biggest breakthroughs to share here with you.

LOVE UNCONDITIONALLY

After much trial and error, I can wholeheartedly say I truly love others, and myself, *unconditionally*. I've discovered some hacks to help relieve a ton of extra disappointments in my life, which is what helped me to experience such unconditional love. These are things I think everyone would benefit from experiencing, so if I may share a moment of your precious time with you, Mama, then let's get growing!

Ever since I was a young girl, I dreamed of becoming a mommy. It's been in my nature to nurture for as long as I can remember. From playing mama to my dolls throughout childhood, and helping with my mother's home daycare; volunteering to assist in the kindergarten classes in my youth, and caring for my thirteen-year-younger sister in my teenage years; and babysitting dozens of children up until today-years-old, I've always loved taking care of children.

Becoming a mother came with an unexpected bonus lesson on unconditional love.

Flash forward to my late twenties—this dream of becoming a mommy was finally coming true, or so I thought. I was just beginning to feel that unconditional love that I heard so many mothers speak about. I was expecting my first baby, and I had mentally, emotionally, and spiritually become attached to the idea of being a bona fide mother nine months later. Unfortunately, I miscarried four months in, and *disappointment* barely begins to describe the first milliseconds of emotions that engulfed me afterward. (*Cue the world's most understated understatement.*)

Miscarriage is something that far too many women have suffered through since the dawn of humanity. I experienced it twice. My heart goes out to all women who lost their babies at any point—I am truly, deeply sorry. I share this because it was an extremely impactful blessing in disguise that gifted me my first major lesson in growth through motherhood, and it led me to a practice that would later serve well in all areas of my life.

With hindsight, I realize that I burdened myself with a tremendous weight of expectations. Upon me being so attached to having a baby, I was literally forced—multiple times, by mother nature herself—to let go. I witnessed many friends and family members having babies year after year, which fueled my expectations as most of them were younger than me. I felt like I was in some unspoken race to the "parenthood milestone," because if I had a dollar for every time someone asked me, *"When are you going to have kids?"*, well, you know what I'd be.

Years prior, a doctor told me that due to my past physical health complications, I would likely never be able to have a baby nor make it to full-term even if I did get pregnant. So, after a pre-cancerous scare that required cervical surgery, and two failed pregnancies later, I came to accept the fact that perhaps the doctor was right. I had no choice but to challenge myself to embrace a new motto of, let go and let's grow! I concluded that growth can only come when we reach beyond our current circumstances. If we aren't growing, we're on our way to dying; there is no in-between. The line that separates growth from death is so thin, "plateau" barely exists at all. There's always *some* degree of a tipping point in one direction or the other. Observing this theory, I began to look at my dark times as little gifts of opportunities to grow because from that point onward, there were no other options in my mind.

GROWING FORWARD FROM HERE

In the game of life, I was level thirty-three when I was blessed with my first rainbow baby. It took my husband and I nearly half a decade's worth of "trying" many things to help us conceive. I can't describe the pure joy and gratitude I felt when I eventually held my healthy newborn in my arms after having a beautiful water birth at home. The love that encompassed me in that moment was unlike anything I felt before. Because of my past sorrows, I was able to appreciate that experience far more than I would have, had I not endured such losses. This was a huge turning point in my life, and I still thank my lucky stars to this day.

Unconditional self-love is a work of heart, and it begins with healing our first child—our inner child—deep within.

Surprisingly, loving my baby unconditionally taught me how to truly love myself in the same light. I previously struggled with self-worth and self-love my entire life. It wasn't until my adulthood that I started doing conscious inner-healing work, and finally began to overcome parts of my struggles. I learned how to be more patient, gentle, and nurturing with myself, thanks to doing the same for my little starseed.

I also realized how children have a magical way of highlighting the parts of us that could use extra love. Whenever we feel triggered by our children (and anyone / anything, really), we can rest assured there's unresolved trauma or something there that needs attention and healing. We cannot be the light without acknowledging the dark. Inner-healing is an ongoing, ever-evolving, empowering journey that I practice regularly with myself and as a coach with my clients. It's like "peeling back the layers of time" and revealing past traumas that yearn to be *peeled and healed* (from this lifetime, as well as generational and ancestral). It's also a removal of conditions and programs that hold us back from experiencing the life we deserve, which is why this work is so important to me in serving others.

As I learn more about my children, I simultaneously learn more about myself.

Children are our greatest teachers in life—we can un-learn so much by observing and emulating the divine qualities they have. They are naturally loving and present in each moment; authentic, carefree, self-motivated, passionate, persistent, curious, resourceful, creative, empathetic, assertive, confident, and innocently ignorant to the negative aspects of life that society and the systems in place imposed upon us. They harbor all of these astounding qualities, until they don't, due to negatively influential or preconceived programming. These traits are something most adults strive to achieve, and guess what: we all once had them! The problem is we're conditioned to cover them up, silence our sovereignty, and dull our shine. Crazy, right?!

Many life-experienced elders make statements on what matters most later in life, and the traits listed above are commonly mentioned. It's as if we were born with the gifts that we end up desiring on our deathbeds—and I'll be damned if I learn that lesson too late in this lifetime! I'm on a mission to un-learn systematic programming, return to loving *unconditionally*, and bring myself back to the basics: with a child-like heart, an unbiased zest for life, and my third eye open.

This brings me to common knowledge that most of us are aware of: change starts with oneself. When we pour into ourselves, we are *only* then able to fully pour into others. We can't give what we don't have, so we must fill ourselves first. Self-love is a term that's tossed around constantly these days, so I invite you to take the time to discover what that means to you. As much as many of us enjoy self-care rituals like bubble baths, pampering, reading a good book (*wink!*), or the like—I believe self-*love* actually runs much deeper than this, and it takes practice and conscious intention to seriously *grow* there.

Just like I came to understand unconditional love because of my babes, I also observed some actions that I believe helped me spread that same love toward others and to myself. In retrospect, there were three key factors that played a huge role in this awareness. I have since been able to integrate this practice into all areas of my life, and I promise it's simple to apply, though easier said than done at first.

Expectations can lead to attachments,
and attachments can lead to disappointments.

When we have strict expectations of desired outcomes, we often become attached to obtaining them. And when we have attachments to expectations that go unmet, we become disappointed. *Boom!* So, how do we rid ourselves of unnecessary disappointments? Think of it like the old "control + alt + delete" sequence on a computer keyboard, which we use when we want to terminate an unresponsive application. When we control our expectations and alternate our attachments, we can in turn delete excess disappointments. I love this simple analogy and how it can be applied to all aspects of life. Let's break it down:

CONTROL EXPECTATIONS

Control insinuates managing, in this sense, and expectations are firm beliefs that something will in fact happen. So, by "control expectations," I mean: "let's manage what we expect." These days expectations are often too high in volume, too low in satisfaction, and well-beyond our control. The expectations I've let go of are from people, circumstances, and things *beyond* my control. This is a very different concept than having a specific set of standards—to which I hold myself reasonably high.

In reality, we have little-to-no control over most things besides our own minds. There are infinite factors and possibilities from innumerable sources that are outside our reach, so a huge lesson I learned was to relinquish most of my expectations and be more open to outcomes. Now, I'm not saying "do not care about anything at all," there's no life or love in that. There's also obviously a time and place where expectations are necessary for survival—like gravity, for example: jump off that cliff and you can expect to fall! My point is the act of trying to control anyone or anything beyond our innate power is un-serving. It's much better to release the inclination to control so much, surrender to the powers that be, and focus on sur-thrival over survival.

When we control our expectations by not trying to control outcomes, a tremendous weight is lifted from our souls and life becomes liberating, exciting, and much more free!

My biggest "a-ha" was learning to let go of the fact that I was literally no longer *expecting* after my second pregnancy loss. I concluded that perhaps it was beyond my control, and I developed a new *healthy attachment* to loving *without conditions*, and explored adoption as an option. I felt excited in a new way! Then, something magical happened a couple of months later. Once I relinquished that pressure and those expectations (and learned to love either way, anyway), we conceived again—and the third time was the charm! Some may call this a coincidence, but I don't believe in those. I'm more of a miraculous synchronicities kind of gal, and I promise you my mindset has been *very* different since then. If there's hope for me, there's hope for *many*.

I invite you, too, to spare your sanity, manage only the minor things you actually *can* control, and learn to let go of the rest with love. Have faith in knowing things will be what they will be, and everything will work out in the end—if not, then it's not the end! Flip the script, and experiment with shifting your perspective to see what works best for you. Keep it simple, try not to overwhelm yourself (or others) with expectations, and just grow with the flow.

ALTERNATE ATTACHMENTS

Alternate, in this case, is another word for alternative, other, and different—pretty straightforward. And attachments, of course, refers to deep and enduring emotional bonds, whether they be to a person, circumstance, or thing. Knowing this, I find it beneficial to choose alternative *healthy* attachments (such as developing security within relationships), and consciously select what we are deeply and emotionally bonding ourselves to—in the best way possible. Healthy attachments are one thing; however, unhealthy attachments are unnecessarily common and can be quite damaging.

In order to love unconditionally we must remove all existing expectations, and unhealthy attachments, and purely love without conditions.

Rather than becoming unhealthily attached to expectations, I again invite you to just love with no strings attached. Harnessing this superpower is like holding sand in the palm of our hand—we end up with more when we don't squeeze *too* tightly. The fewer expectations we attach ourselves or hang on to, the fewer chances we have of being disappointed when things go awry (which, as we know, they likely will at times), so the less, the better—amiright?! Modify unnecessary attachments, and remember: nothing is permanent—change is the only constant.

DELETE DISAPPOINTMENTS

This is the cherry on top! I believe it's possible to delete a massive portion of our disappointments in everyday life by renouncing our overall expectations and attachments. Of course, it's inevitable that disappointments beyond our control will arise. However, I know from personal experience it is possible to avoid most of our common dismays by trimming the excess.

Having fewer expectations and attachments gives me greater peace and happiness, because I appreciate more with less.

Unfulfilled expectations usually cause disappointments. So, if we get to the root and remove those expectations (again, referring to the unnecessary "extras" here), then we can potentially save ourselves a ton of excess disappointments. It's one thing to have faith, hopes, and dreams—I'm a huge advocate for all of these! I also know they are very different from expectations and attachments. If anyone wants to delete any amount of disappointment from everyday life, the fastest and most effective way to do so is to let go of controlling expectations and unhealthy attachments. Period.

EMBRACE THE UNEXPECTED

I invite you to contemplate which areas of your life you can apply this "control + alt + delete" method, and truly love without expectations, too. What if things work out better than you think? What if you could steer clear of avoidable stress, headaches, and heartbreaks in life? What if you could save time and energy from being spent on worry and wondering?

You were never meant to carry the burdens of the entire world—you already have enough on your plate as it is, Mama.

The Universe never gives more than we can handle—it sends us exactly what we are ready for at the exact time that we need it in our lives to grow. At the end of the day, there are positives in the negatives that we can learn to embrace if we trust the process. By releasing the weight of expectations and attachments to outcomes beyond our control, we can expect more calm and peace in our lives; more balance and satisfaction; more clarity and focus; more happiness and joy; more *unconditional love*; and much, much more.

Without expectations, my will is for you to consciously follow your intuition, grow to be your best self-advocate, and love your way through life. May you be as conscious, compassionate, and care-full with yourself as you are with your babes. There is only one you, dear Mama. You *can* expect to believe you are the world to your children—and I hope you turn that love inwardly as well. Please gift yourself that same unconditional love that you so truly, deeply deserve.

With love, light, and blessings,

-Krysta Lee xox

Chapter Nine

Rediscovering Yourself After Motherhood

"Nurturing the child within means making
a conscious effort to always give your inner child
the space to be creative, to connect to themselves
and others, and to share their story."

Emanuela Martina Hall

EMANUELA MARTINA HALL

ig: ig: @emanuela_speaks I fb: @EmanuelaSpeakingCoachandActor

li: Emanuela Hall I yt: Emanuals Speaks

Emanuela is a speaking coach, actress, teaching artist, and mama of two, residing in Hamilton, Ontario. She is passionate about helping people connect to themselves and others through creative expression and storytelling. With her company, *Creative Wellness*, Emanuela leads interactive performing arts workshops that promote healing, health, and connectivity for people of all ages, demographics, genders, and backgrounds. For over a decade, she was the Creativity Coach for an assisted living facility where she led mindfulness, arts, and movement programs for residents and staff.

In 2019, Emanulea wrote, directed, and starred in her award-winning, one-woman play, *My Breast Self*, about the challenges of new motherhood. This experience helped her release her own story, brought her back to her home on the stage, and connected her to so many local mamas with similar experiences. As a speaking coach, Emanuela loves helping entrepreneurs and executives find their own captivating voice and magnify their presence, so that they can make an even bigger impact.

Emanuela is a 300-hour registered yoga instructor, a graduate of the American Musical and Dramatic Academy, and has her BFA in Musical Theatre from The New School University (NYC). She loves espresso, prosecco, long summer days, Christmas, traveling, and hearty laughter around a delicious meal with loved ones.

Rediscovering Yourself After Motherhood

Who's your inner child? What are they doing, and what do they need from you?

This question, asked during a visualization exercise in my *Creative Wellness* workshop, is often followed with emotional release. Several mothers in the room discover that, over the years, their inner child has been buried or completely ignored. Many have a difficult time with this question because they spend their days pouring themselves into nurturing their children. While this type of devotion to our kids is important, forgetting to take time to care for our inner child can lead to parenting in a way that feels disconnected and overwhelming. Losing yourself in motherhood is a common story I hear from moms time and time again. It doesn't have to be this way. I want you to know that it *is* possible to be an awesome, devoted mother *and* feel like yourself. You don't have to sacrifice one for the other, and you don't have to trade in your inner child for the responsible adult.

Let's make one thing clear: no matter which way you slice it, motherhood is a struggle—there's no perfect way to do it. I'm by no means a parenting guru, but what I've learned is that unless we start with ourselves, we'll never live up to the (often unrealistic) expectations we've made for ourselves. Taking care of the child within means remembering yourself. Remembering who you were and who you wanted to be. Life will throw us curveballs, but that doesn't mean we can't be kickass moms *and* be ourselves too.

> *Motherhood does not have to be the thing that takes you away from yourself, it can be the thing that takes you back.*

Connecting to your inner child, creativity, and sharing your story, are vehicles to get you there.

Let's go back to when we found out we were pregnant. No matter what that looked like for you, I bet you spent the next forty weeks or so obsessing over what to eat, how you *should* or *shouldn't* labor, and the kind of delivery you envisioned (among other things). Perhaps you made a registry to ensure you'd have all the items required for a baby in the modern-West (carrier, car seat, noise machine, etc.). An incredible amount of time and money went into making sure your body and home were ready to welcome a new life into this world. We parents-to-be are so busy reading the books, taking the classes, and buying the stuff that many of us forget to notice the other life that is being born into this world—the new version of us! The day we become parents, our entire *being* changes. Our body changes, our heart changes, and our lifestyle changes. Most of us are too busy to notice these changes because keeping a baby alive is damn hard! It's only once we pause to notice how anxious, lonely, or "different" we feel, that we realize we are also hard to keep alive.

When I was pregnant with my first son, I wanted to do it "naturally;" no drugs, no intervention, skin-to-skin, breastfeeding for a full year, the whole deal. I assumed I'd done all the right things. I took prenatal classes, I read sleep books, I had midwives who knew my birth plan. Still, things didn't go *at all* how I planned. At forty-two weeks, I still wasn't in labor. We decided on an induction and, after forty-eight hours in labor, my cervix still wasn't dilated, or as I liked to say, it "wasn't doing what it's supposed to." We went for a C-section. It took five days for my breastmilk to come in and, after a lot of pressure from the nurses, when my baby's cries sounded like he'd been living in the Sahara for months, I finally gave him formula. Then I went to my bedroom, shut the door, and cried my eyes out.

The sense of failure and shame that surrounded my birth story is not unique. Sure, sometimes plans don't work out, but feeling like we don't have the right to talk about it, is worse. Whether we get the birth of our dreams, or the complete opposite, moms who are blessed with a healthy baby and safe(ish) delivery are told to "be grateful." Well-meaning family members, in an attempt to help, remind us of how much worse it could have been if _____ (you get the idea). My disappointment and sadness weren't worthy of complaint.

After those early days of motherhood, the fog starts to clear. You begin sleeping, wearing your normal clothes, and maybe go back to work. On the outside, we seem to be the same person. Most of us are too wrapped up in our child to acknowledge the shift within us, and we ignore the pieces of us that we're grieving. What is absolutely clear is that the person who existed before motherhood (whether or not you had a child biologically) is not the same person that exists now. If you feel like a part of you died when your child was born, then you're not alone. Of course, we must let go of certain parts of ourselves to allow space for a new (and improved) version—but not the parts of ourselves that we loved, not the parts that make us feel alive. Those parts can stay. Taking steps toward rediscovering yourself in motherhood, nurturing your inner child, and finding your people, will help you to feel whole again while making you an even greater mom.

The process of healing and reconnecting to yourself has three parts: finding your inner child and new-self, creative expression, and sharing your story.

Let's begin with the first step. The simplest way to reconnect to your inner child is through a **guided visualization**. Block twenty minutes of time for yourself and find a quiet place to get comfortable. Rest one hand on your belly and allow a quick exhale out of your mouth, releasing all your breath. Allow your breath to enter through the nose, filling your lungs. As you inhale, push your navel into your hand, imagining the breath filling the belly like a balloon. Exhale on an open-mouthed "ahh." Repeat this until you feel your body relaxing completely.

You can pre-record the following mediation on your phone and play it back to yourself. Pause between each sentence to give your mind a chance to fully visualize each line:

Allow an image of yourself as a child to arise. Any age that comes to mind is good. Look at the child in your mind. Look at the hair, the eyes, the mouth, the expression, the clothes, the body position; take in all of your child. That child wants something from you, something that you are able to give . . . Look at your child. Your child needs something from you. Now it's time to give that child what it needs—whatever it is asking for, give freely. Now it's time to physically take care of your child. Take the time that you need now to do for your child. Look at that child and love that child. Your child needs something from you that you are giving it now. Take some time to nurture and give to your child... Whenever you feel ready, do the last things you need to do, or whisper the last things you need to say to your child. Let your child know that it is safe and that you will be back to visit again. Slowly allow your attention to return to the room, and whenever you feel ready, you may open your eyes.
(Drama Games by Tian Dayton, PhD)

Take some time to journal or draw a picture of your visualization. This can be very powerful, so practice self-compassion and talk to someone if you need extra support.

Whenever I do this guided meditation, I can clearly see my six-year-old self; pink velour romper, long, dirty-blonde hair pulled back in tightly-wound 80s style "bobble" elastics. Sunglasses on, hair-brush-turned-microphone in hand, standing on our fireplace performing Madonna's "Papa Don't Preach." This is me; confident, sassy, and craving the spotlight. It's always been me, and many parts of that little girl are *still* me. (I'd give anything to wear bobbles again, if they're still a thing in 2021, please let me know where I can get some.)

Journaling is another useful practice that connects you to your inner child and your new self. If you're thinking, *Journaling? I'm not that nerd*, then hear me out. Putting your thoughts on paper gives them less power over you. An article in PsychCentral.com, *The Health Benefits of Journaling*, noted that "writing removes mental blocks and allows you to use all of your brainpower to better understand yourself, others and the world around you."[1] It goes on to list "know yourself better" as one of the many benefits of journaling. It doesn't have to take up too much time; jot down your thoughts before you grab your phone in the morning, leave a notepad by the shower (the best insights come to us there), or keep a gratitude journal by your bedside. Try your best to get your "thinking brain" out of the way, and simply write any and all thoughts that come into your mind.

My favorite way of getting in touch with myself is by getting into my body either with yoga, hiking, dancing, or working out. This is how I physically release things that are weighing me down or causing me stress. If you do nothing else, commit to moving your body every single day. I promise you will start to discover your ability to manage life as a mother will improve.

The second step in the process of rediscovering yourself after motherhood is **creative expression**. I would argue that creative expression is essential at every stage of life and, when I say creative expression, I don't mean *artistic* expression. Art is a tool humans use to express ourselves, but creative expression comes in many forms; cooking a meal without a recipe, gardening, or rearranging your office are all ways you can activate your creativity. Creativity has the power to bring us into the present moment. Neurologically speaking, creativity builds new synapses (or information channels) in the brain, and it has been linked to higher levels of dopamine, otherwise known as the "happy" neurotransmitter. Creative expression has also been linked to increased immune function.[2]

---

1 Maud Purcell, "The Health Benefits of Journaling," ed. Scientific Advisory Board, Psych Central, May 17, 2016, https://psychcentral.com/lib/the-health-benefits-of-journaling#1.

2 Ashley Stahl, "Here's How Creativity Actually Improves Your Health," Forbes, July 25, 2018, https://www.forbes.com/sites/ashleystahl/2018/07/25/heres-how-creativity-actually-improves-your-health/?sh=656f78a013a6.

Creative expression will give you a way to find your spark again, to find that piece of you that you haven't had the time to nurture.

In her TEDx talk, Cristina Riesen points out that, "If you deny yourself creativity, you become underdeveloped. You start to create a narrative in your life that will be pleasing to the world around you, but you will feel broken inside."[3]

When I was six months postpartum, I wrote down my birth story; from the moment I found out I was pregnant to the moment I stopped breastfeeding. I wanted to document it, though I had no intention of doing anything with it. After my second child was born, I felt even more overwhelmed and lost. I was suffering from postpartum insomnia and baby blues. I lost my zest for life. Through the inspiration of a life coach, I decided I would spend twenty minutes a day turning my postpartum story into the one-woman play, *My Breast Self,* which I performed at theater festivals. I didn't know it at the time, but this act of creative expression did three things for me; it helped me heal, it reignited my passion for performing, and it connected me to other moms. This little play helped me come back to that little girl with the bobbles and hair-brush microphone.

This brings me to the third and final step in rediscovering yourself after motherhood: **sharing your story**. When we share our story, it validates it. Sharing our story connects us, raises us up, and can give a voice to those who may not be able to share theirs. Think of a time when you felt completely recharged after an intimate conversation, a good book, or a riveting film. Stories move us, and yes, everyone has one. You have the power to help others find themselves by sharing yours. You don't have to write a play, or post on social media, or become an author. We are all called to share our stories in different ways. Through your process of rediscovery, your unique way of sharing your story will become clear to you. Maybe it's the story of that time you helped someone at the grocery store and became best friends. Or it's the story of all the things you find hilarious in the world. Or maybe it's the story of your trauma. Whatever the story, whatever the medium, your stories need to be shared to fully express who you are.

The process of self-discovery is . . . a process. It requires consistent practice and a dedication to wanting, above all else, to find your spark again. I can assure you, it is worth every minute and every dollar I've ever

---

3 Cristina Riesen, "Plea for a Daily Creative Act from TEDxZurich," www.youtube.com, January 19, 2017, https://www.youtube.com/watch?v=2qkfnkZ6ZO4.

spent. How do you stay consistent and continue to unpack the beautiful story that is you? The tools I shared are keys to unlocking your new self, but connecting to your community is the lock those keys fit into. Perhaps this sounds like a daunting task at this stage in life, but you *can* find your tribe. Take up a new skill (or an old one) and meet people at a class or workshop. Find an online community where people with similar interests and passions hang out. Try searching Facebook groups, or find coaches running programs that interest you.

Imagine what it would feel like if motherhood was easier. Imagine having more energy, more calm, and less resentment. Imagine being a happier mom simply by being *you*. The new and improved you who hasn't forgotten their inner child, or things that light them up. I invite you to try some of these practices in your life—try implementing one new thing each week or month. Eventually, you'll find a ritual that feels manageable, and you won't know how you did life without them. My rituals are non-negotiables for me because I know they make me a better mom; I am less reactive, more joyful, and more present.

> *Taking care of me also sets an example to my kids for how they can take care of themselves, too.*

There is no perfect way to rediscover yourself after motherhood. What matters is that you do it. What would it feel like to find your spark again? Remember, your flame is still inside you. It's always been there. *You* are the only person who has the power to ignite it.

Chapter Ten

Can't Have One Without The Other!

"Sometimes the best dreams are the ones
you don't know about yet."

Jaime Hayes & Marnie VandenBroek-Hookey

JAIME HAYES &
MARNIE VANDENBROEK-HOOKEY

www.HelmetFreeLife.com
ig: @helmet.free.life | fb: @Helmetfreelife

We are two women in completely different places in life. Through all of our differences, we are still able to meet in the middle. This is such an important place for us because it's where the rest of the world melts, and we can be just us. While being opposites, we are both drawn to helping women embrace themselves. Our differences allow us to support women to achieve their best and embrace their uniqueness. Our journey began in second grade, where a tomboy and a wallflower grew up to be the women we are today. It's rare to see friendships lasting thirty years, and here we are, living our best lives. We have not always walked the same path; however, we have always found our ways back to one another. From childhood friends to wild teenagers, to wives, to mothers, and becoming entrepreneurs; overcoming tragedies and being grateful, for it all only could have come from one thing: GROWTH!

Can't Have One Without The Other!

This is our story and how our leap into growth started with a simple doughnut. Have you ever wished you could turn your love of doughnuts into something more? Well, we found a way to do just that with our Instagram page, *The Helmet Free Life.*

Don't worry, we both wear helmets when needed. For this to make more sense, we should start at the beginning.

Sarnia, Ontario has a population of only 74,293. Jaime moved from Wallaceburg, Ontario, and Marnie from Wyoming, Ontario, towns even smaller than Sarnia. We both moved to Sarnia in 1987, not knowing each other until our first day of school in second grade, and this is where our journey as friends began. Throughout elementary and high school, we stayed consistent friends, and some years were stronger and better than others.

Marriage, motherhood, jobs, and just life, in general, got busy, but we ALWAYS stayed in touch. In 2010 we became close again, and at a coffee shop in 2018 is when we decided to put our lives "out there" and begin an Instagram page called *The Helmet Free Life.*

Let us introduce ourselves: Jaime is a full-time real estate agent who has attention deficit disorder, which often leaves her mind wandering. Her busy mind, love for homes, and attention to detail sparked her career of selling homes. Real estate allowed her to build a career around her passion for match-making people with their dream homes and build some amazing relationships along the way. Marnie, over the years, has owned a couple of different businesses, and about five years ago, made the decision to be a stay-at-home mom and raise her blended family of five children. Marnie went through some life-changing hard times, and through those hard times, she felt alone and isolated—even though she had so many people around her trying to offer their support.

"The support felt distant, like I was drowning while everyone offered sympathy from the safety of the shore. I realized that I could learn more through a tear than a telescope and began to expose my pain and suffering to others. This opened my eyes to a community that allowed others to relate, and hopefully understand that they too can move past the pain, feel the feelings and that they don't have to stay in the box that society has created around grief."

Marnie began sharing and supporting others through their own pain and began to think of how impactful it would be if she shared those lessons and what she has overcome with others. She came up with the idea that a blog could be a platform to share this with others in her community. "I decided to go to the one person who not only saw my darkness but climbed down the rabbit hole and sat with me until I was ready to see the light. She was the one who never judged me or my pain. I couldn't think of anyone more fitting than Jaime. I decided to approach her to be a part of this blog in hopes to show others how powerful it can be to experience and express your emotions with the support of others. Taking care of myself led to the ability to change my perspective, and it allowed me to find joy in life again. Through this joy, I began sharing my journey with others and found the power in shining a light on grief, as opposed to suffering in the darkness."

The *Helmet Free Life* page is a lifestyle Instagram account created by our lifelong friendship. Becoming some sort of an influencer was not a career choice for either of us. As our kids got older, we found ourselves with more time on our hands and a feeling of wanting to do more. We both were wondering how we could make a bigger impact on not only our own lives, but also the lives of those in our community. In 2018, some time had passed since we last spoke, as it had many times over the years of our friendship, and we always decided to meet up for coffee to catch up again. We ended up chatting for hours, just laughing so hard our faces hurt, and then our crazy thought to collaborate and create the account was born.

This page allows us to express our own thoughts and experiences with our community.

We had no idea of all the avenues and opportunities for growth it would bring us. We simply wanted to make a difference, and we wanted to support others in their path of growth—the same way we have been able to support one another throughout our lives. Being with each other through the highs and lows, we are now able to offer that support to so many more people. Through exposing our own pain and suffering we have highlighted what people can overcome together.

Not without its challenges, *The Helmet Free Life* has created a space for us to grow in the most unexpected ways. We were raised in homes where creative dreams and emotions weren't really fostered or supported. Jaime's childhood had doubt and a lack of support. From an early age, we were both placed in a "box," feeling trapped and limited. We both experienced a similar emptiness, that only parts of us would be approved by those around us. Never having experienced a sense of unconditional support and acceptance, we felt unheard. This page allowed us to find a new community of individuals who saw us as inspiring, which gave us encouragement instead of doubt.

In the beginning, Jaime almost backed out of the blog, and that's when Marnie offered to go for a walk with her to discuss what she was going through. What was supposed to be an enjoyable walk through a wetland trail near our homes, began a muddy and treacherous walk through puddles deeper than we had dressed for. Marnie's goal was to show Jaime that if she could begin to talk through her discomfort, as opposed to suppressing it deep in her gut, healing could start to occur. Jaime expressed her concerns about opening up and exposing herself to people she didn't know. We talked so much that we forgot all about how muddy it was, and that suffering together loosened the strings—as opposed to continuing to feel suffocated. Our walk began with clean clothes and cluttered minds and finished with mud everywhere, smiles on our faces, and light in our souls.

As we all know, with growth comes some growing pains.

When the page became increasingly known throughout the community, Jaime started to revert back to her old insecurities. She is a natural introvert and was not used to being in the public eye this way. Her past did not prepare her to openly share her emotional experiences and insights with others. A deep fear of judgment and negative response rose to an unbearable level for her and almost pulled her out of the page completely. "I was so uncomfortable with my life being put out for whomever to see and began sorting through my life, thoughts, and feelings—which is extremely difficult for me. When I was younger, I always envied others; I hated myself, and I always wanted to be someone else. Through our page, I have really appreciated finding my true self and worth. I have learned and embraced that I do not want to be anyone but me! I am now able to be the person to look up to for others, a position I never imagined myself holding. I still have many emotions to sort through, but every day gets easier."

The Helmet Free Life account has allowed Jaime the incredible opportunity to understand her own path to growth. She has found new comfort and confidence in expressing her emotions and experiences with their followers. "I can confidently say I am exactly where I am supposed to be, and this page has allowed me to feel a sense of pride and accomplishment for things and parts of me that I used to shy away from and judge." Nothing grows in our comfort zones, and Jaime decided to lean into the discomfort—and continue to live a "Helmet Free Life."

In July of 2010, Marnie was a thirty-year-old woman with two young children, not knowing her life was about to change forever. "My husband died very suddenly in the middle of the night while I was sleeping beside him. I woke up to a sound I will never forget, in a moment that I felt would never end. By morning light, and from that day forward, my life came crumbling down. This was when my true growth as a woman started, as I had so many choices to make for not only me, but for my two children. I began my journey making many mistakes along the way, but I also made some amazing choices as well. In time, my heart and mind began to heal, which opened me up to love again—and that led me to meeting a wonderful man with three daughters who had also lost his wife to cancer. This was when I realized, life gives us second chances, opens us up to growth, and it helped me find my purpose. I want to share my hardships with others to help them grow from hard things and to understand that life is happening *for* us, not *to* us."

Now, remember when we mentioned this all started with a doughnut? Our page took on a life of its own following the creation of "The Helmet Free Doughnut," which laid the foundation for us to notice that people and businesses were watching us and wanted more! The buzz throughout our community echoed so rapidly for this doughnut; they would sell out within a couple of hours.

This incredible doughnut came to be when Jaime was experiencing a lifelong struggle of only finding heavy cake doughnuts filled with dense whipped cream. She started buying Krispy Kreme doughnuts because she loved how light and fluffy they were, and she would cut them in half and fill them with her homemade fresh whip cream. She would rant to her husband Justin about why couldn't something like this be made up at a doughnut shop?! Justin eventually felt compelled to approach our local bakery to see if he could surprise Jaime with a small batch of her dreamy doughnut creation. The bakery agreed, and he couldn't wait to stun her with his thoughtfulness. Marnie saw Jaime post this loving gesture on *The Helmet Free Life* story and rushed over to try them. Upon taking her first bite, Marnie determined everyone needed to try this incredible doughnut!

We then approached the bakery to make us two dozen doughnuts that we could share with our followers in order to get their honest opinions on it. After an afternoon of randomly meeting up with followers and getting their first taste "live" on our stories, The Helmet Free Doughnut became an instant hit—and everyone wanted to get their hands on one.

A few days later, we got word that there was a tray of "The Helmet Free Life Doughnuts" in the bakery's showcase window! We were so excited that we had to see this for ourselves, and together we raced over to the bakery. There it was: OUR DOUGHNUT!! We thought this would be a temporary thing, but a year and a half later, it's still selling strong!

The unexpected celebrity status of "The Helmet Free Doughnut" sparked the interest of other local businesses to reach out to our page to share and promote their products and services with us. Since then, we have been busily working with other local businesses, including clothing stores, salons, breweries, and more. We have helped so many local businesses grow through our platform by allowing them exposure to customers who never knew of them before.

Our page began to blossom into not only a place for us to share our lives and insights, it also became a place to share local products and services that our community has to offer.

For Jaime, the connections with businesses and followers offered a new source of passion and connection in life that she could not have imagined finding. Having businesses value us is something that has brought a humbling calmness of fulfillment neither one of us was expecting, along with a newfound confidence that we both had been lacking.

As our page exploded with popularity, so did the amount of work associated with it. The success of this page could not have been accomplished without one another. We are best friends who could not be more polar opposites, but it works. Jaime is the organized chaos who can set goals and ensure each step is taken to guarantee success. Her experience with real estate has allowed her to obtain a skill set of ensuring "tasks most-hated" are met on time. Marnie is the creative and emotional soul who has an innate ability to express and share her thoughts with the world in beautiful and insightful ways that connect our followers on a passionate level. We balance each other's strengths and weaknesses perfectly and can pick up where the other has left off.

Through sharing our own uniqueness with our community, we were able to spark the growth of others—and that, to us, is everything.

Marnie was invited to be on a podcast and be the opening speaker at a women's social event. "This invitation not only excited me, it also left me paralyzed with fear. A goal of mine has always been to share my story with honest and vulnerable emotion. This was my chance to share in front of two hundred fifty women. I took a deep breath, walked on stage, and began to share my life-changing story. As the words I spoke left my mouth, the fear that was deep in my stomach was soon replaced with confidence and enthusiasm. Not only was I able to face my biggest fear, I was also able to fulfill a dream and share my story with others. When I finished, I looked into the crowd to see Jaime giving me a standing ovation, which brought tears to both our eyes. This truly was a milestone that will never be forgotten."

Our collaboration has opened more doors than we ever could have imagined. It has brought growth within ourselves, our friends, our families, and our jobs. We would love to see it continue to grow and create a positive impact for even more people. We want to continue to use our *Helmet Free Life* as a platform to celebrate life, motivate and inspire others, and support others in their own journey of growth.

Opportunity is everywhere if you are willing to open yourself up to the possibility of failing, and still be "all in." Life has always given us two options: to step forward into growth, or step back into safety. We hope you choose the first one like we did . . . *GROWTH!*

Section Three

Shifting Lifestyles:
Conscious Choices

*"Being a mother is discovering strengths
you didn't know you had, and dealing with fears
you never knew existed."*

~ Linda Wooten

FEATURING:

Lisa Kern
Jessi Harris
Susan Elstob
Sandy Casella

Chapter Eleven

Mama's Gotta Slow In Order To Grow

"Be grateful for all of it: The highs.
The lows. The blessings and the lessons."

Lisa Kern

LISA KERN

www.healthyholistichappy.com
ig: @Holistic_ot | fb: @Lisa Kern

Lisa Kern is an eternal optimist with an open mind and heart. Her spectrum of interests runs wide, and she has a deep-rooted belief that you should follow your heart and intuition at all costs. She considers herself a student of life with a passion for personal development, health, and wellness.

Lisa has a master's degree in occupational therapy, and a bachelor's in science from American International College. After working for ten years as an occupational therapist specializing in neurological rehab, she chose to follow her passion and true purpose: working as a holistic health and wellness coach, empowering others to live their happiest and healthiest life. She is now focused on building a brand to empower others to optimize healing from the inside out—addressing body, mind, and soul.

As a multi-passionate entrepreneur, Lisa also holds certifications as a brain injury specialist, yoga instructor, Reiki practitioner, and is co-founder of Work Your M.O.T.O.R., an online home exercise program for stroke survivors.

Lisa lives in Western Massachusetts with her husband, Bill, and two children, Will and Gavin. Skilled at seeing the silver lining in situations, Lisa's personal mantra is, "Without struggle, you will never know your strength."

Mama's Gotta Slow In Order To Grow

The timeliness of this chapter is ironic because, in a sense, the COVID-19 pandemic of 2020 has us all shifting our routines and adapting to a "new normal," but noticeably, many people had a hard time embracing the change of pace and slowing down. Our society for so long has made us believe that happiness comes from success, and success is obtained by accomplishing, doing, earning, and producing. The real epidemic then, is the number of mamas suffering from burnout, fatigue, anxiety, and being overwhelmed. We give and give but don't know how to receive.

While slowing down to speed up sounds like a contradiction, consider the idea that some of the world's most well-known athletes and performers all embrace a mindfulness practice and understand the value of slowing down in order to speed up. It's the idea that we require rest, renewal, and space to relax to be more patient and focused so we can remember how to experience life and not just react to it.

Growth, by definition, is the process of developing or maturing physically, mentally, or spiritually. When I work with clients, I like to give the analogy of a four-legged chair, each leg representing a part of your being: physical, mental, emotional, and spiritual. If one of those is out of balance, then the chair is naturally not as stable. In our busy Western culture, we spend a lot of time focusing on our physical bodies, but we often neglect our mental health and spend even less time nourishing our emotional and spiritual needs. We go, go, go until our physical bodies make us slow down. We are conditioned to do more, learn more, make more, and have more in order to feel successful and fulfilled.

But pause for a moment to think about that. What does it mean to be fulfilled? What is your definition of success? Now, I realize that this answer will be different for everyone, but I ask you to stop for a second and write down what it means to you. A quick Google search will tell you that being fulfilled is a process through failures and victories, rather than focusing on one specific moment. A fulfilling life comes from building habits that lead to joy. We are then, as Aristotle said, "what we repeatedly do."

So, it comes down to our daily habits—they can make us or break us.

Habits can help you be productive and happy, or majorly suck your time and energy. As a mama, what do you need more of? I'll answer for you in case we are on the same wavelength: *time, peace, patience?* So, how do we cultivate this in our already too busy lives?

Before we dive into tips that will facilitate growth in these areas, first thing, Mama, pat yourself on the back. You grew a freaking human (if not within your body, then you are still raising them), and care enough about them to pick up this book to better yourself. Huge air high five! Then, ask yourself where the idea came from that you always need to be productive and why it never feels like enough? This is the reason I chose to share my story. It took me decades to realize where my false beliefs came from.

When I was fourteen years old, my mother was diagnosed with terminal cancer and was given six months to live. I can vividly remember the day I received the news. How I hated my father for being the messenger and how I ran for hours until my lungs nearly gave out—I couldn't breathe or feel anything. I decided in that sad, helpless moment that my mom would not see me cry; I would not show weakness. I couldn't wrap my head around how hard it would be for her to prepare to leave her husband and three children behind. *I would be strong for her.*

To avoid the inevitable feelings of grief, anger, and despair, I pretended like it wasn't happening. I went to school like my world wasn't crumbling at home; I showed up to softball practice like I didn't have a constant pit in my stomach; I hung out with my friends, never acknowledging my fear that my life would never be the same. My mom, bless her tired soul, didn't know how to bring up the subject, my brothers were master avoiders, and my dad started drinking again. We just kept going.

At some point over the years, I confused strength with stifling hard emotions. I completely gave up on my faith and stopped going to church because I couldn't wrap my head around the kind of God who would make someone be without a mother. I also ruled out talking to a therapist because, well, I was a teenager, and I didn't like the approach of the abrasive hospice nurse who wanted to talk about my mom dying. I would be strong on my own. I would make my mom proud and excel at everything to prove to her and the world that I would be okay. I would put one foot in front of the other and be fine. *I'm fine, everything's fine* became my motto. Unconsciously, from the moment I got the news, I made myself busy and suppressed my thoughts, cluttered my mind, and avoided dealing with the crippling sadness of losing a parent. *Shove the feelings away and stay busy. I'm fine.*

I've grown a lot since then, but some patterns are difficult to unlearn. Staying productive and busy was always a coping strategy, but it took me decades to realize my patterns. Can you relate to staying busy to fill a void or feel like you are in control when the world around you is so unstable?

Through years of personal development work, I learned that it's very common for people to attach their self-worth to their productivity; hence the need to always feel like you have to prove something to someone. If you are feeling like you can't get everything accomplished in a day, chronically running on empty, have everything you could possibly need but still feel unfulfilled; I promise you the answer is not to do more, but to do less. If you are feeling stuck, unsatisfied, or like you have lost your "oomph," Mama, hear me out . . . you will speed up your momentum by slowing down.

This chronic need for busyness caught up to me in my thirties. I was checking all the boxes and chasing all the accolades, achievements, and results—but I was drained and unfulfilled. Then I would feel selfish for these thoughts—making me feel worse.

Mel Robbins, American TV host, author, and speaker preaches it best and teaches that busyness stems from fear and that staying busy makes us feel like we are in control.

When you slow down, you get honest with yourself. Ask yourself these questions:

- What are you running from?
- What is your soul trying to communicate with you?
- What do you really want in life?
- What are the things that you are filling your life with that aren't serving you?
- Where can you slow down and free up time to make progress on things that matter to you?
- What is the feeling that you are after?

"Voluntary simplicity means going fewer places in one day rather than more, seeing less so I can see more, doing less so I can do more, acquiring less so I can have more."
-John Kabat-Zinn

TIPS TO SLOW IN ORDER TO GROW

These are the actual principles that helped me find more peace, gain clarity on my purpose, and decrease my daily anxiety.

How to G-R-O-W (Gratitude, Rise Early, Observe, Welcome Joy)

Tip #1 Gratitude

In the wise words of Oprah, "What you focus on expands, and when you focus on the goodness in your life, you create more of it." If you believe at all in the law of attraction or manifestation, this is precisely it. If we think negative thoughts, the universe will deliver negativity. However, if we think positive thoughts of love, thankfulness, acceptance, and gratitude—we are letting the universe know this is what we want and are welcoming more of into our lives.

This can serve as a reflection also. What lessons are you grateful for?

Be grateful for all of it: The highs. The lows. The blessings and the lessons.

A mentor once asked me to think about the worst thing that has ever happened to me and then think about what beauty came from it. To apply it to this story, the worst thing would be my mom's death. I immediately got defensive and thought that absolutely nothing good happened from that. But in fact, a wonderful thing happened. Because of our history and my beautiful mother's diagnosis, I had to be screened regularly for cervical cancer. Sure enough, when I was thirty-six years old, cancerous cells were detected, and I had a hysterectomy. I can now watch my children grow because of it. I learned to be grateful for the time we have and to tell people I love them because tomorrow is not promised. By expressing gratitude daily and *slowing down* to appreciate the little things, you will be happier and more fulfilled.

Tip #2 Rise Early

Even if you are not a morning person, for the love of everything holy, wake up before your children and enjoy that precious hour of alone time with a cup of coffee or tea to set your intentions for the day, pee in peace, and work out. Move your body for 20-30 minutes, get that shit done before any other excuses come in, and you will absolutely feel better because of it.

Robin Sharma, Canadian writer and brilliant leadership expert, speaks about the power of a morning routine to increase productivity, rest, and joy. It is in these quiet, meaningful hours to ourselves that we can listen to our desires and reset, rest, and move our bodies in order to tap into our creativity and potential by quieting the noise before the chaos of our daily routine sets in.

Rise early. Breathe. Slowly embrace the day and move your body.

For years I have worked on conditioning myself to wake before the sun rises, finding beauty in the mundane, and I cherish this time to myself before my kids (and even my husband) wake up. It's become my sacred time to pursue my desires and interests. *My only superpower is consistency.* I try to show up for myself every day at least for an hour because if I am depleted, and my cup is not full, then no one else can benefit. My youngest child is an early bird, like me; I swear he has a radar that goes off as soon as I sit in silence to have my morning coffee. Routinely, I would bribe him to go back to bed, yet he would persist. I found this bittersweet, so I let him stay. The workout I choose is a quick, high-intensity video because I like to sweat and get it over with. Five minutes in, my son unrolls a yoga mat and practices his taekwondo kicks next to me. I realize in this moment that kids are wildly more impacted when they have a role model. He sees me practice at life. He sees me struggle and pause my video because I can't keep up. I'm teaching him in these moments—every rep, every drip of sweat—that persistence and resilience matter. He sees me push through and tell myself out loud that my mind will quit before my body. In this moment, he is doing as I do, not as I say, and I find this to be profound.

So then, what if a responsible mother is one who shows her children vulnerability and struggles? My children do not benefit from me shielding them from hard things or learning that things come easy. My children benefit from seeing the work, the search to find myself. They are observing the idea that we are all works in progress and that is more than okay.

Tip #3 **Observe**

Observe your thoughts and hang out with your soul—aka: meditate. When you sit in silence, magical things happen. You get downloads from the universe, and your ego steps aside to make room for your soul to speak. You will get to know your core desires and remember what you were placed here to do. If you are like me and believe that your mind is too busy to meditate, then that is the exact reason to begin a meditation practice. Remember, meditation is not the absence of thoughts, it's simply a process of resting the mind in its natural state, and observing emotions and sensations in your body.

If you feel the need to speed up, slow down.

If nothing else, the act of sitting in silence will bring you more clarity, peace, and a sense of calm to be able to deal with the chaos of life and motherhood. We as adults set the emotional tone for our children; if we are calm, they will reflect it. If we are stressed and chaotic; they will mimic this as well. Meditation is one of the most useful things you can do for yourself and it's free! It will help you grow, gain patience, self-awareness, creativity, and perspective.

Tip #4 **Welcome Joy**
When this clarity was coming and I started to slow down, I was introduced to a beautiful soul named Jennifer Jayde, who would later become my spiritual mentor. One of the things she teaches is to follow the breadcrumbs of joy.

Ask yourself these questions:

- What lights me up inside?
- What is the message that I get excited to share with the world?
- What can I talk about for hours on end and feel inspired by?

It is your unique gifts and abilities that make you happy, that you should share with the world, and that will allow you to grow and feel fulfilled. Don't overthink this or wonder how you will get there.

Just follow the spark and do more of what makes you happy in this moment.

This is where many people get hung up on staying in an unfulfilling career or relationship. The dreaded word *should*: I *should* be happy with where I am; I *should* stay in this dead-end job because it's the responsible thing to do; I shouldn't take that course because it's too expensive; I *shouldn't* leave my unhappy relationship because I'd have to start over. And the never-ending list goes on, stops us in our tracks, and prevents us from taking the leap toward something that could bring us total joy— all because we are stuck in fear.

Sometimes, as we grow older, our passions and values change, but we are so invested in our lives that we feel it's irresponsible to change our minds or try something new. Your breadcrumb might be remembering that as a child, you loved to dance or draw. Maybe the next step is finding an adult dance class or buying some drawing supplies. This may end up being a great pastime or could turn into you changing careers and opening your own dance studio to feel alive again. It doesn't have to be this dramatic, but the idea is that you let go of the attachment of where that trail will lead you and simply follow the things that bring you joy in this moment.

The beauty of motherhood is in the process.
Slowing down to enjoy the small moments that
light us up, bring us joy, and fulfill us.

I invite you to think about the feelings you want to experience, such as peace, love, and connection. I'm not implying that you don't have to work and make money—money is necessary for living—however, you are not here on this earth to "just accomplish." I believe we are spiritual beings having a human experience. We need to take care of our physical bodies, as well as our mind and soul because we are human be-ings, not human do-ings. You are here to live and enjoy the ride. Abraham Hicks says, "The basis of life is freedom. The purpose of life is joy. The result of life is expansion."[1]

This is your permission to slow down and enjoy it as much as possible so you can experience expansion. Grow, Mama, grow.

---

1 Abraham Hicks, "The Basis of Life Is Freedom," www.youtube.com, January 21, 2018, https://youtu.be/0yP4OxJap9E.

Chapter Twelve

Where You Are Is Not *Who* You Are

"You have everything inside of you to get started creating the life you were meant to live, and to step into the remarkable person you were meant to be."

Jessi Harris

JESSI HARRIS

ig: @jessi_r_harris | fb: @jessi.harris.796
li: Jessi Harris | tiktok: @jessiharris78

Jessi's mantra is "life on fire". . . and despite divorcing when her children were two and five years old, Jessi never let that fire in her heart go out. Struggling to raise two boys, Jessi worked full-time as a nurse, taught first aid, and also contracted herself to universities to aid in research studies. She did whatever it took to keep hockey skates and football cleats on her boys' feet. In 2017, Jessi was introduced to personal development and entrepreneurship and hasn't looked back since. Working hard to grow herself and master the skills required to reach her goals, Jessi has completely transformed her life and inspired many people in the process. She recently incorporated her business and took a leave from nursing while she completes her master's and pursues her business goals. Jessi believes we rise by lifting others, and she strives to breathe belief into women—and help them see that no goal is too big; rather, we simply underestimate the work required to achieve it.

Where You Are Is Not *Who* You Are

Before I share my story, I want you to stop and take a minute to thank yourself for showing up. Thank yourself that, despite whatever is happening or has happened, you are choosing to grow—choosing to do the work and become the best version of yourself. Secondly, really absorb this next point: I want you to know, without a doubt, you are amazing. You are wonderfully and beautifully made—your worth is not determined by your bank account, your pant size, your kids' school grades and behavior, or your marital status. You are enough, and already have everything within to reach your goals and create the life that you deserve. And despite circumstances that may sometimes seem overwhelming, *where* you are is not *who* you are. How do I know that? Well, I guess that's where my story begins.

I grew up in a little town on an island off the east coast of Canada called Newfoundland. I lived with my mom, dad, brother, and sister in a little log house on a salmon river. When it would rain, every pot and bowl in the house would be used to capture the water leaking through the roof. In the winter, we would have to leave the water running so the pipes wouldn't freeze. It might not sound great, but growing up in our little town was the best childhood ever. Our tummies were always full, we played outside all day, and my parents always did their best to support us. I remember my mom and dad fighting a lot, though. I think that's what solidified in my mind that I needed to get an education; I needed to be able to provide for myself and future children, and never be unable to leave a situation I did not want to be in.

After high school, I went straight to university and completed two years at the Memorial University of Newfoundland. My dad moved to Alberta for work, and my parents eventually separated. I visited him during summer break from university and fell in love with the Rocky Mountains; I transferred to the University of Alberta, where I completed my Bachelor of Science in Nursing with Distinction. I was the first person in my family to have a university education. Shortly after moving to Alberta, I met my (now ex-) husband. Looking back, I can see how my need for external love and validation set the foundation for our unhealthy relationship.

As humans, we have a unique ability to see people for who we want and need them to be, not who they are.

What I wanted more than anything in the world was to be loved—which eventually led me to tolerate years of emotional and mental abuse. I always thought someday he would wake up and think, *Wow, I'm the luckiest guy in the world*, and would never be mean again. That didn't happen. If you are in a relationship like this, please know this is not normal and, chances are, it is not going to get better. We cannot fix others; we can only heal ourselves. When the boys were two and a half and five years old, I found out that my husband was having an affair. The emotions ranged from the deepest pain and betrayal I had ever felt, to an overwhelming sense of relief that it was finally over. Like a semi-truck had been lifted off my chest.

You see, I've always been a high achiever; I always finish what I start. So, no matter how bad my marriage was, I don't know if I would have ever walked away. The person I am today would have, but I don't know about the person I was then. He never came home again. I was left to pick up the pieces, figure out how to pay the bills, a mortgage, and raise the boys. I remember sitting on my bathroom floor crying, and at that moment, I made a decision: *where* I am is not *who* I am. No matter what, I was going to do whatever it takes to ensure that my boys and I are okay.

I switched to a permanent night shift so I would make an extra five dollars an hour and so I could work while the boys were sleeping. I would get home in the morning, wake them up, and get them off to school. Then, I'd sleep for a few hours until it was time for them to come home, spend a few hours with them, have supper, do homework and baths, and get them ready for bed before my neighbor's daughter would come over. I would then leave for work, and she would put them to bed. My mom and dad had since reconciled, and they were instrumental in helping me raise the boys. Additionally, when overtime shifts became available, I would work extra hours, but it still wasn't enough. We were falling further and further behind financially. I took a course to become a first aid instructor, and I opened my own small business teaching first aid and CPR on my days off.

I remember that first Christmas I was on my own with the boys. I didn't have any extra money to buy Christmas presents, but I had my diamond engagement ring, my wedding band, and a diamond tennis bracelet that I received for my wedding. I went to a local pawn shop and traded all of my diamonds for cash to buy presents for the boys that year. It was worth it on Christmas morning to see the smiles on their faces. Diamonds can always be replaced, but special Christmas memories with my boys cannot. The boys and I spent a lot of time outdoors biking, hiking, skiing, kayaking, and camping. We had a lot of fun together. Behind closed doors, I was stressed financially, though—living check to check.

A few years passed by, and when the boys were six and eight, I eventually started dating a friend we had met kayaking. He loved hanging out with the boys and me. I thought this was finally our happily ever after. A year after we started dating, we made the decision to buy a quarter section of land and move out of town with plans to marry and have more children. Life was good. Until it wasn't. I came to learn that he had a temper and that his ideas around parenting and discipline were very different from my own. Again, at that time, my need for love and validation caused me to see what I wanted to see and not who he really was. There were so many warning signs that I ignored. This eventually led to my son being assaulted and charges being laid. We packed our things and moved; we were starting over again. My name was on joint assets, campers and vehicles, and it took two years and cost thousands of dollars in lawyers to settle the farm and our joint assets. Once again, I was financially devastated.

I reminded myself where I am is not who I am.

I contracted myself to universities on my days off, worked overtime, and did whatever it took to provide for the boys and myself. I needed to find a way to earn more income, so I decided to go back to school and take my master's to become a nurse practitioner.

During all of this, my oldest son was diagnosed with type 1 diabetes. For those of you who have or have had a loved one with type 1 diabetes, you'll understand that it was a devastating diagnosis. I grieved the loss of a normal, healthy life for my child. To this day, I am committed to finding a cure for this horrible disease in my lifetime. I remember that moment like it was yesterday. We were in the emergency room, Izayah was lying in the bed, and they told us his diagnosis. They gave him his first dose of insulin, collected blood, and put an IV in his arm. He was twelve years old. He was lying on his side, not saying a word; silent tears ran down his cheeks.

I asked him, "What are you thinking?"

"I'll never play hockey again," he replied.

I took out my phone, and I said, "Okay, let's look up NHL hockey players with type 1 diabetes." We googled it and found out that Max Domi was an NHL hockey player with the same diagnosis.

I said, "Okay, what's something else you've always wanted to do?"

"Be an Olympian," he said.

I quickly replied, "Okay, let's look up Olympians with type 1 diabetes."

Again we searched and found that there were multiple Olympians with the same diagnosis. We continued this process over and over, until we found that everything he ever wanted to do in life, someone with type 1 diabetes had done it. I told him, "From this moment on, you cannot control that you have type 1 diabetes, but you can control what you let it take from you."

In life, there are many things that happen that are beyond our control, but we are always in control of how we react and what we let it take from us. Where we are is not *who* we are.

Within a year of Izayah getting diabetes and us moving again, I was introduced to the world of personal development and home-based business. This is where my life really started to change. I started to learn that my outside world was really a reflection of my inside world. I started to accept responsibility that every situation and circumstance that I continued to find myself in was a reflection of patterns that I had created. Patterns like the one I had mentioned earlier, a need for external love and validation. It was empowering to understand that we have the ability to change those patterns. It really starts with changing our thoughts and our emotions, and choosing ones that serve us.

We have the ability to create our future, and it starts inside—regardless of our environment.

I turned my vehicle into a mobile university. I stopped hanging around people that were not in line with the new me I was creating. I stopped watching TV. I started reading books, and listening to podcasts and audiobooks. I was recreating who I was. I was choosing to be the person I wanted to be. I started to let go of old habits and old ways of thinking. My time was intentional. In 2018, I found a business mentor and got to work. I spent the next two years obsessed with getting better in all aspects of my life. I cast a vision for my future. Every morning I would spend time alone in my thoughts, creating joy and living out my future in my mind. I started a gratitude journal where I was not only grateful for what I had, but also for everything that was coming. I created an abundance mindset and celebrated the wonderful life that was ahead *before* it ever showed up in reality.

Happiness is a choice. It starts inside, and it is not dependent on outside circumstances or environment. Nothing has to happen for us to be happy; it is a choice. During this time, my environment would continue to challenge me. You need to understand, though, that challenges are opportunities for growth. Adversity is meant to bring out the greatness in us. We need to develop our minds so that regardless of the circumstances, we can rise above, rise out of our situation, step into our greatness, and step into the power that is within us. We need to understand that situations do not define us, and our only limitations are the ones that we create in our minds. Every single day we have two choices: stay the same or grow. When we take responsibility for our lives, good or bad, it gives our power back to us so we can find solutions. When we blame people and situations for our life, we give our power away.

Our subconscious mind cannot tell reality from make-believe. So, if we start to tell ourselves we are worthy; we are strong; we are successful; we are wealthy; we are generous; we are loved; we are kind; we are a leader; we empower women to live their best life; we are unstoppable; our mind does not know the difference. We get to choose the movie we play in our mind, day after day. We get to choose the story we listen to. Why not choose one that serves the future you? In the beginning, it may not be true, but our mind doesn't know that. If you do this every day, then you *will* start to make choices that are in line with that future version of yourself. You will start to attract people that are in line with that future version of yourself. You will start to attract experiences that are in line with that future version of yourself, and then, one day, you will wake up, and you will be living in that life you created in your mind. It starts inside, though, long before it ever shows up on the outside, and you need to back it up with work.

Anyone who works with me has heard me say: everything worth having is uphill. When you decide to change your life, know that there will continue to be challenges—but your *will* needs to be so big that nothing can stop you from becoming all that you are meant to be. I remember hearing Tony Robbins at *Unleash the Power Within* in LA. He said, "One of the biggest problems with people is that they think they shouldn't have any problems. Problems are a gift, they are an opportunity to grow. The only people without problems live in graveyards, so you should be thankful to have problems, it means you're alive."[1] I'll add to that: if you're alive, it means you have another chance.

> *You have another chance to create the life you want—to become who you want to be, and to live how you have always wanted to live.*

Now, I sit at home writing this story to share with you, and my life has completely transformed over the last couple of years. I recently took a leave from nursing, I'm completing my last course in my master's, and I work from home full-time in my business. I have zero credit card debt or loans, and for the first time since I divorced 13 years ago, I have savings and investments. The boys and I are starting to live a life that I had

---

1 Tony Robbins, "Unleash the Power Within" (March 18, 2019), https://youtu.be/mB54G7OPSHk.

created in my mind when my circumstances would have made it seem impossible. The boys and I have a great relationship with their dad and his wife. I'm inspiring and helping other women on their own growth journey, both inside and outside of business. One by one, I'm helping them see that *where* you are is not *who* you are, and that your past does not dictate your future. You have everything inside of you to get started creating the life you were meant to live, and to step into the remarkable person that you were meant to be.

Chapter Thirteen

Your Life Is Your Story To Write

"I want to look back on my life one day
and be really proud of the story I wrote."

Susan Elstob

SUSAN ELSTOB

www.islapearl.com
ig: @islapearllife | fb: @islapearllife

Susan Elstob is the face, voice, and vision behind the *Isla Pearl* brand, with an unwavering commitment to empower other women to find their confidence through personal growth and style.

What do friends and colleagues say about her? "If you hang out with Susan for long enough, she'll have you believing in just about anything—especially yourself."

WHO AND WHAT WE ARE SUPPOSED TO BE

I t was the moment my daughter walked over to me and said, "I want to own a bakery AND be a dance teacher, because bakers work early in the morning and dance teachers teach at night. That way I can do two things that I love." She was probably six or seven years old at the time, and as the words "you can do and be anything you want" fell out of my mouth, I also was hit with the realization that what I was telling her was very different from what I was showing her.

For decades, I had been climbing the corporate ladder. With every level I reached, the additional dollars on my paycheck and perks that came with the title took me further away from why I started working with senior citizens in the first place. But that's usually how it happens. We start something because we are drawn to it, maybe even passionate about it. It fits us at the time. But as we grow, change, and evolve—so does our purpose.

I started working with seniors at the age of sixteen and quickly fell in love with it. Hearing their stories, and helping them in whatever way I could—and in many ways, being the company that they needed. I was fortunate to work amongst a team dedicated to transitioning people through one of the most difficult times in their life. I felt fulfilled in my work. I felt like I was making a difference, until I didn't anymore. What I can now see looking back, is that the further I moved away from why I got started working with senior citizens—to help, support and guide them through a challenging stage in their life—the further I also moved away from my purpose.

I spent the last few years of my career in a pretty low place. Between struggling with fertility on and off for years, hopping on a plane to fly across the country, or driving up to five hours a day just for a quick meeting—I knew something needed to change. But I had worked too hard to "get here." I mean, on the outside looking in I had it all. I had what we are all told to work for, and what success looks like. I had the career, title, paycheck, bonus, office, travel—all of the things that by society's definition equaled success. The problem is that I was depleted, on the verge of breakdown, and the furthest away I had ever been from feeling like myself. I spent most days daydreaming about what my dream job would be: working in style, buying, personal growth and development, yoga. All things I loved that inspired and fueled me, but definitely not a job description that was anywhere to be found. So I kept pushing through, losing pieces of myself every day because I couldn't give up everything I had worked so hard for. Everything that I was "supposed" to be.

THE DAY IT ALL CHANGED

This was the day it all changed for me. Like one of those moments that stops you in your tracks and you are forever changed. A moment that leaves an imprint that you can't ignore. In the middle of my "want to be a stylist, buyer, yoga teacher, personal growth leader" identity-crisis, I headed out to visit one of the retirement homes I supported in my role. I was always drawn to this home because of the magic I felt when I walked through the doors. It was full of innovation and vibrancy, and a team with equal energy. Looking back on it, I am not surprised that a team and home I was always so drawn to ended up being the one that changed it all for me.

The thing about working with senior citizens is that routines are very well established. You run into the same people in the same places doing the same things. That day was different. The energy was different. Outside of the dining room that day was a giant whiteboard. I mean, this wasn't different—it was always there filled with information, reminders, and maybe a joke of the day. Except on this day, only one question was written:

What would you have done if you knew you would not have failed?

It stopped me in my high-heeled tracks. I mean, here I was a thirty-something year old with very little life experience in comparison to the life stories that were standing in front of me. Obviously, I was late for my meeting, as I stayed a while to watch the board fill up with answers. And that it did. Responses like "get married again," "have children," and, "become a pilot," flooded in as I watched the board fill with unfulfilled dreams, and something inside me shifted.

Something inside me changed the way I looked at my life and how I had been living it. It was like a scene from a movie where you watch your life summarized in a thirty-second clip. The theme? I was always choosing safety, security, and what I thought I was *supposed* to be doing—instead of what I *wanted* to be doing. Living this way, under these self-imposed rules and beliefs (with a little extra help from society), had led me off course—so far away from who I wanted to be—and more importantly: who I could become. Short story? This moment and these residents opened my eyes to living a life without regret. Working with seniors is what made me step away from working with seniors. Like a sign I wasn't even looking for.

WRITING A NEW CHAPTER

It was about a year later that I decided to step away from my career. I knew that I wanted to write a different story for myself and my family. The problem was, somewhere between starting my career and leaving it, I had also lost some of who I was outside of my titles. I was in a full-blown identity crisis, not knowing who I was or what my next step would be. But I also knew that I needed to take ACTION. Being unemployed or being a stay-at-home mom has never been part of my DNA, nor was not having a paycheck to contribute to the financial realities and dreams of our life.

The clock was ticking, and I needed to make a move. So, I went into the task thinking about (and making numerous lists of) all the things I could do. And just as quickly as I started to bring an idea to life, my subconscious would kick in and tell me how ridiculous I was. I was a phone call away from going back to my old industry and secure ways when my husband asked me, "If you could do anything—create anything—what would it be?" And then, the floodgates opened as if it had all been sitting there waiting to be unleashed, like my baker-by-day, dance-teacher-by-night, six-year-old daughter.

I wanted to create something that inspired and empowered women. With events, and social gatherings, and style, and real talk, and, and, and . . .

My husband's response to this was, "Well, it doesn't make sense to me at all, but it sounds like something you should do because you've put a lot more thought into this than you probably realize." That's the thing. As much as we think we are consciously living our lives, there is this silent narrative that runs behind the scenes. We pick up inspiration and pack it away. We hear words that resonate with us. Not only that, but we see someone who sparks something in us. These moments are just that—moments—and we're often too busy living our lives on autopilot to realize that these moments are trying to wake us up to what our real-life story should be. These are the "white board" sign moments so many of us are looking for, we just don't have our eyes open wide enough to see them.

I knew that if I wanted to write a new chapter, I had to start a new page. One that was unlike anything I had done before. I knew that I needed to step away from the safe, secure, and status quo if I wanted to create something big, bold, and fulfilling. That was the moment my brand and business *Isla Pearl* was born. Names that not only connected my two grandmothers and my daughters. Names that represent a side of confidence and boldness, but also filled with laughter and warmth. The mission: to have women leave feeling better than when they arrived, whether it be through a conversation, caption, video, or message.

That was literally all I had: a vision and an idea. I didn't have a plan, and I certainly didn't have it all figured out. I was a thirty-something-year-old mom, in full-blown identity-crisis mode, conflicted between not wanting to be a full-time career working mom, or a full-time stay at home mom. I was motivated to get going but didn't know where to start (sound familiar?). So, I started with what seemed easy and achievable. I secured my domain name ☑, chose a WordPress theme ☑, (also aging myself), chose my font style and color ☑, and then started to write, and write, and write. I had never considered myself to be a writer, but the words just seemed to flow out of me like they had been bottled up for years.

Every single day after dropping my kids off at school, I would sit at my computer and write about whatever I was going through, how I was feeling, or whatever inspired me that day. From seeing someone out running in the rain, to a chance encounter with a stranger, the words continued to pour out of me the same way they did when my husband asked me that game-changing question. It was as if they had been stuck—unsaid, unwritten, and unspoken—building for years, and just waiting for permission to be released. Those words? They created almost one hundred blog posts. Blog posts that sat unpublished behind a domain name and pretty landing page that no one could see. Yes, unpublished. Because hitting the publish button made it real. And making it real meant that I would be opening myself up to what others might think, how they might judge me, or what they might say—probably not to my face, but definitely behind my back. Fear based on hypothetical people saying hypothetical things. Sounds like a logical thought process, yes?

This went on for almost six months. Sitting down every day to let the words and thoughts out, without opening myself up to share them. Because *what if?* The kind of *what-if* dialogue that is dramatic enough to win an Oscar. The kind of *what-if* dialogue that stops us from taking a chance and has us clinging to safety and security like a life raft. The kind of *what-if* dialogue that has the potential of writing our regrets on a white board one day. Our mind does this to keep us safe, protected—and, in my opinion—small.

These "what-if" statements hold us back at every opportunity they get.

From letting ourselves daydream, to letting our ideas become our reality, to writing a new chapter that reads nothing like the last one. Safe and secure was not going to lead to the big, bold, and fulfilled life I wanted to write—so I decided to flip-the-script on my *what-if* statements to be ones of *abundance*. What if I *did* create what I wanted to? Or do what I wanted to do? Who would I become, who would I be, who could I help, and who would I inspire to do the same?

HIT THE PUBLISH BUTTON ON YOUR LIFE

I hit the publish button and the floodgates opened. Someone who once-upon-a-time never considered herself to be a writer, found herself on "Top Blog" lists alongside some of the biggest names in the industry. Someone who almost didn't hit the publish button out of fear of what others might think.

What are you sitting on and thinking about right now that you aren't allowing yourself to go after? What do you talk yourself out of? Where are you staying stuck, safe, and secure? My friend, if you do anything—create anything—what would it be? And I'm going to add something to this, that I now know is the real by-product of going after what you want: who would you become if you did?

We tell and encourage our kids to do and be anything they want, without giving ourselves permission to do the same.

We encourage them when they are struggling and remind them that working hard will show results. We believe in their wildest dreams and will do anything to make them come true. But when it comes to ourselves, we fall short. We let the *what-ifs* hold us back, and doubt and fear become stop signs instead of yellow lights. We fail to even get started because of how we might be seen and judged, instead of leaning into that confident six-year-old version of ourselves that is still sitting there below the surface.

Five years after getting started on my new chapter, I now show other women how to do the same. To find their confidence, to find their stride, and to figure out who they want to become. You were someone before you became their mom, and my friend—that person matters. She might be right there below the surface, ready and waiting for permission for the words and dreams to flow out of her, or, she might be found layers deep below, living under expectations and definitions of success that were not meant for her. This is *your* life to live, so write a story that feels good to you without worrying about what anyone else's chapters and books sound like. You will become who you were always meant to be, and your children will see what it means to go after whatever they want in this life and to bring their dreams to reality, too. Only you (and a few pre-teen TikTok stars) can do that. Not through your words, but with your actions.

YOUR LIFE, YOUR STORY

Your life is your story to write. You don't need to become an entrepreneur, leave a job or career that you love, become a social media influencer, start a side hustle, or turn what you are passionate about into a full-blown business. You just need to start leaning into what fills you up, what leaves you feeling at your best, and choose whatever it is that gets you one-step-closer to being the person you want to be—outside of being a mom or any other title that you have.

My friend, you were someone before you were their mom, and although you might be different from who you were before that title got added to your repertoire, you are *always* evolving and growing. New chapters are always being written. You just need to decide what you want to write, and what your story is going to be.

Chapter Fourteen

Find Your Tribe, Find Your Voice

"I believe the best thing we can do for ourselves and our children is to trust our instincts, and raise children who are allowed to voice opinions; be the individuals they are; and make their own choices and mistakes."

Sandy Casella

SANDY CASELLA

ig: @casellahomesrealestate | fb: @CasellaHomesRealEstate

li: casellahomesrealestate | tw: @Sandy_Casella

Sandy Casella is a Real Estate Broker, Investor, Author, Emerging Public Speaker, and Philanthropist. She began investing in real estate at the age of twenty-two, and later found herself starting life over again at the age of fifty—after becoming single, broke, and in debt. She is a mother of three children, grandmother of two, and is currently writing her first solo book—which will be released in the fall of 2021. Her goal is to be a change agent in the world of mental health and wellness, and she believes we should leave this world a little better than how we found it. Sandy resides in the beautiful small town of Lynden in Ontario, Canada.

Find Your Tribe, Find Your Voice

I knew I wanted to contribute to this book as soon as I saw the opportunity. I knew my answer would be yes, but it took me a long time to reach out and ask about it. The hesitation to inquire was because I had no idea how, or what, I could contribute; I felt like this was a book for a younger generation of women who were raising young children. I thought *there must be something I can offer*, based on my experience of raising (who I believe to be) very strong, independent people—adults who contribute very much to this world. I would like to take full credit for that, but I think while I have taught them on some level, they have individually taken what life has thrown at them and become the amazing people they are today.

I had my first child at twenty years old, and at that point, I had only held one other baby in my life (my niece, who was born eleven days prior). To say I was scared to death would be an understatement. I had no idea how to care for a baby, but what I did have was an incredible amount of love for this beautiful child. I had never felt that intense of a bond before in my life, and I just knew we were going to be okay. I had two more children after that birth—my second five years later, and my third eight years after that—making my first and third children fourteen years apart. My husband and I had made a conscious decision to spread the births of our children out because we read that if children are more than five years apart in age, the second child is more likely to have the traits of a firstborn, and you can possibly avoid "second child syndrome." In case you are curious, I don't think it worked!

After having my first two children, I knew I wasn't ready to call it quits. I knew I still wanted another child, but my husband and I weren't ready at the same time. It took a few years for us to be aligned, and when I got pregnant with my third child (who, for the record, was not an "oops" child), she was very much planned! It's surprising to me how many people ask me this question, and also ask if they all have the same father—so to clarify, they were all planned, and all have the same father.

Their father and I were in a complicated relationship for thirty-one years; it was a physically, psychologically, and sexually abusive relationship—and it took me many years to find the courage to leave. I won't get into the specifics, but what I do want to touch on is what finally gave me the courage to leave and why I'm telling this story.

*"You can't connect the dots looking forward;
you can only connect them looking backwards.
So you have to trust that the dots will
somehow connect in your future.
You have to trust in something—your gut, destiny, life, karma, whatever. This approach has
never let me down, and it has made all
the difference in my life."*
- Steve Jobs

I'm not writing my story for pity; I'm sharing it because I am "connecting the dots backwards" now—thank you, Steve Jobs, for that analogy. I didn't understand his theory for many years, yet now I see how *and why* I was eventually able to acknowledge that what was going on in my life was *not* okay. For many years, I couldn't fathom how to connect the dots backwards, but now it all makes sense. As you look back on your life, you can actually see the pivotal points that helped you to grow and change. I can now see the specific events and people that came into my life and helped me to understand what I was feeling inside (but could not mentally grasp at the time), which was the fact that my relationship with my husband was not healthy.

I made the decision to leave the marriage after I realized that I was modeling a very unhealthy relationship and I did not want any of my kids to end up in the same type of marriage. How could they ever be in a healthy relationship if they didn't even know what a healthy relationship was?

Throughout my relationship with my then-husband, I often wondered why I didn't have the courage to leave or to stand up for myself, but I now see it's all part of the psychology of control—and what finally made me realize that *women have a voice* is what follows here . . .

When my daughter was in elementary school, I was involved in her school's fundraising activities and the parent-teacher group. This was a safe place for me to go to, and my husband oddly let me get involved—he had controlled everyone I spoke to or associated with over the years, but this didn't threaten him for some reason.

While doing this, I became good friends with a group of women who, to me, were extremely powerful. I was intimidated by the fact that they all had university educations, whereas I had dropped out of high school at sixteen, and didn't have any post-secondary schooling. I did eventually obtain my grade twelve equivalent through correspondence courses, so I didn't feel like a *total* failure. Sometimes, when they got into conversations about their post-secondary experiences, I would physically excuse myself because I didn't want them to know that I had dropped out at sixteen. They were also in (what seemed to be healthy) marriages, whereas I was just in a common-law relationship and had never married legally—which I didn't want them to know about, either. (On one hand, it was a mutual decision by us not to get married, but on the other hand, I was ashamed of it.) And to top it all off, all of these women at the school were stay-at-home-moms, and I was a working-mother . . .

To paint a bit of a backstory leading up to this point in my career, I had played a supportive role in my husband's businesses for the better part of the first years of our marriage, and although I held a real estate licence, I wasn't working full-time in real estate sales. I also contributed to our real estate investing business, and later in a car repair and sales business. During the times when I wasn't contributing to the household financially, my husband would continuously say the money was *his* money, and he made it clear that it was because of him that we had income—and that my part in the businesses was not valued. Then when I did contribute to the household financially, for many years, I was told that the money I earned wasn't *my* money, even though I was responsible for paying all of the bills and supporting the family. I accounted for every penny and rarely spent much on myself, other than the necessities.

Now going back to the moms at the school, every Wednesday morning, I would have breakfast with this group of women. I was totally in awe of the fact that they were stay-at-home moms, and they got to go out for breakfast, spend time on themselves, and pay for breakfast with money that was not "*theirs*," according to my then-husband's beliefs. I struggled for years to *earn* this kind of luxury, and it wasn't until I was involved in my real estate business and earning *extra* money, that I felt that I could treat myself.

These women would plan cross-border shopping trips and buy themselves clothes and items that to me were not "necessities;" they would also get their nails done, and some even had cleaning ladies who helped them at home. I'm sure you can imagine what was running through my mind at this point. I started to realize that what they were doing was normal, and my existence was not. Watching them began to change my belief that "every woman lived under the same circumstances as me" into the fact that what I was experiencing was not only not the norm, but also not healthy. And in reality, it was abuse. I realized that these women had come to a conscious and powerful decision with their husbands that they would raise their children. They were all smart, powerful, bright lights who had left careers and chose to be at home with their children—and their husbands supported them in that decision. I realized that they weren't spending "their husbands" money, they were taking care of themselves so they could be the best possible mom that they could be.

This started to plant the seed in me that I too could be a powerful woman and that relationships were mutual—and both parties supported each other.

These women became my role models, and I started to question everything I believed up to that point. It is now almost twenty years later, and we are still great friends. Some from that original group have left, and a few have come to join us over the years. While we don't have breakfast every Wednesday anymore, we do still have "coffee therapy" mornings, and spend a girls' weekend every year away together. Most of these women don't know what they mean to me or how much they helped me in my personal growth—though they will when this book comes out, which I'm grateful for. We have shared many ups and downs over the years; we have cried together, we have spent weekends together, shared recipes, strategies, stories, and successes about our children—but most of all, we have laughed together and supported each other. None of us could have known the power of this group when we first began getting together. My daughter still marvels at the fact that even though the kids of everyone have not remained close, we, the moms, have.

If you looked at everyone in our group, you would think that we all have it together and that life is great. Everyone has a great relationship with their spouse, and all of our children are doing amazing—but what I would like to share is this: everyone has a story, everyone is dealing with something that you have no idea about, and that woman you know who looks like she has "all her shit together," probably doesn't feel that way. Someone is looking at you right now thinking you are the woman that has it all—whether they see the great husband, the great kids, the great house, the career, the looks, the body—whatever it may be. That doesn't necessarily mean it *feels* that way to you, however.

Whatever we are going through, we can help each other by sharing our stories *and* our struggles. If you have someone in your friend group that makes you feel inferior and puts you down, you need to end that relationship and walk away. If that person is your spouse and they refuse to listen to you and invalidate your feelings, you need to make a decision on who you are going to love more—them or you. Having children exasperates this issue, and I chose to stay in a very harmful relationship because I thought that as long as my kids were not being physically abused, we were all better off where we were, together. I have come to realize that even if you are not being abused but are witnessing it, it is still a form of abuse and trauma.

As women, we can all support each other with every decision, and we can empower each other in whatever choices we make.

Whether we choose to stay at home and raise our kids, or pursue a career as a working-mother; choose to breastfeed, or not; as moms, we know what is best for our children *and* ourselves, and sometimes there is a lot of pressure from the outside to conform to what others think is right. Women who work outside the home should support the women who choose to work *at* home, and vice versa. Both sides of this coin are hard, the guilt of leaving our kids with someone else every day is heart-wrenching sometimes (let's let go of the guilt!), and the feeling of losing ourselves because we left a career is equally hard. Family dynamics have never looked more different than they do today; single women having children, same-sex couples raising children, single men raising children, stay-at-home moms, stay-at-home dads; there are so many exciting opportunities to follow your heart today. By choosing to get to know others, you open up to such great friendships, opportunities, and new ways of looking at things. These powerful women in my breakfast club have taught me so much, and I am so grateful for having met them—and for them allowing me to be a part of their lives—they have helped shape me along the way. They allowed me to find my voice and taught me to trust my instincts.

I invite you, too, to find your tribe. You will know you have found them when your soul feels nourished when you talk to them, when you feel empowered to take on the world after a get-together with them, and when they support you in whatever decision it is that you make. If they don't make you feel this way, then they aren't your tribe—keep going, you will find them—you will feel it in your soul.

Powerfully choose what you want your life to look like, and make *no* excuses for it. Only *you* know if staying at home is right for you and your kids, and only *you* know if even having kids is right for you. What others say about you and your choices are opinions, not facts.

Section Four

Embracing New Normals:
Growing Forward

*"The fastest way to become a fearless mother
is to give up the idea of doing it perfectly—indeed to
embrace uncertainty and imperfection."*

~ Arianna Huffington

FEATURING:

Abby Creek
Teresa Sturino Schiavone
Angel Kibble
Sonia Dong
Tamara Trotman

Chapter Fifteen

How to Find Your Superpowers (When You Can't Even Find Your Cape)

"The paradox of parenthood is that you often feel all of your emotions at once; happy and sad, joyful and tragic, exhausted and exuberant. The key is in wading through it all to find the moments that lift you up. When you do, hold on to them, and the darkness will soon fade away."

Abby Creek

ABBY CREEK

www.wellnesscreek.ca
ig: @wellnesscreek | fb: @wellnesscreekco

li: Abby (Creek) Hildebrand

Abby Creek graduated from Capilano University's Theatre Department in 2005 and has since worked as an Actress, Arts and Sciences Teacher, Hospitality Supervisor, Marketing Coordinator, Admin Director, Executive Assistant, and Wellness Advocate.

Having been a published author at the ripe old age of ten (okay, so it was for a poetry contest, but still!), she has woven the soul of her story into her many careers, and despite being only 5'2", has had the opportunity to flex her growth muscles on all of these journeys, most notably in the newest role of mama.

Her mission is to empower others to take control of their emotional and physical health, and to help them build a path through wellness, one step at a time.

Abby currently resides in North Vancouver, BC, with her quintessentially Canadian husband, Brock, brave and beautiful daughter, Elizabeth, and handsome fur-baby, Capone.

How to Find Your Superpowers (When You Can't Even Find Your Cape)

Girl falls in love with a boy; they have a miscarriage. Life continues.

Girl gets pregnant again years later and gives birth to a gorgeous babe. Girl develops debilitating postpartum anxiety; she doesn't know how to succeed in this new role.

Girl is afraid to ask for help, she doesn't know how, and she feels she doesn't deserve it.

Sound familiar? Because my story may be your story. But don't worry, it has a happy ending.

HAVE FAITH MAMA

Despite being Type A, everything great that has ever happened to me came from taking action without knowing the plan. Being bullied in school taught me a lot about how to keep moving forward, even when I didn't want to. On particularly hard days, my mom would recite to me Samuel Beckett's infamous line, "I can't go on, I'll go on." It used to drive me crazy. "MOM! Don't you see I'm in pain here?! I CAN'T GO ON!" Of course, I could, and I did. It was the end of my final high school year when it became clear that I couldn't go to my dream university, and I didn't have a backup plan. I, self-proclaimed Type-A hyper-planner, didn't have anywhere to go come September. So, along came another opportunity to practice moving forward, even when I didn't know where I was going: *Fine, I'll go into the Arts until I figure out what the heck I'm doing with my life. I don't have to have this figured out today (but tomorrow would be nice).*

> *I learned how to take action in the face of fear and create joy along the way, despite the uncertainty.*

I struggled for years to find something I could settle into, and when I would get particularly restless, my now-husband would remind me, "You don't always need to know the plan." *Hello, have you met me?* But I trusted him, and so life continued.

In the coming years, many of our close family and friends experienced huge losses. We went to five funerals over the course of two years, some of them anticipated, some of them not. And then it was our turn. Over the course of one weekend, we found out we were pregnant, then not. It didn't seem fair. We had already experienced so much loss that year, how do we even begin to process losing someone we didn't even know we had? I would go back to my mother's wise words, "I can't go on, I'll go on." But it was hard. Pregnancy hormones were still flowing through my body like crazy, which in turn made me *feel* crazy. I would have to pull my car over because I was crying so much that I couldn't see. I didn't know how to talk to anyone about it. I didn't even know how to talk to my husband about it. I thought the problem was me—I was the one who failed. And even though my conscious mind knew that wasn't true, my subconscious mind was telling me all sorts of horror stories. *You'll never be able to have a baby. Your body wasn't designed for this. You don't deserve to have a family.*

The only thing that pulled me out of this vicious cycle was the encouragement of my partner—our life was amazing, with or without a baby, because we could handle anything together. He was right, and everything great that had happened in my life was not part of "the plan," so I had to trust that there was a lesson in this also.

WHAT YOU FOCUS ON, EXPANDS

Until I got pregnant the second time, I didn't really understand anxiety. I would hear people talk about their anxiety and panic attacks, but I didn't understand how anxiety could ever stop someone from doing something. There had certainly been times in my life when I was afraid to do something or when I didn't feel qualified, but it had never STOPPED me from taking action. I would embrace (read: swallow) my fear and take action anyway. And then, I started growing a human inside me, and I noticed these "anxious tendencies." We would be at our ultrasound, and I couldn't breathe until I heard the heartbeat. Or I'd lie in bed at night playing out conversations of how to tell our family that we weren't pregnant after all. And although I understood *why* I was on this anxiety train, what I couldn't do was convince my mind to get off. I remember when I was at my midwife appointment a month before my due date, and they asked me to confirm my birth plan. I didn't have one; I just knew what I didn't want.

> *I hadn't learned about the power of positive thinking yet, because everything I didn't want happened.*

Elizabeth was born early Christmas morning. She came in fast and furious—the same manner with which she approaches everything now—and suddenly, I was being prepped for an emergency C-section. So, there we were, having to abandon the "birth plan" basically the minute we entered the hospital. "Abby, things are progressing, and we're going to have to break your water, ready?" *Actually, that's the opposite of my birth plan, but go for it.* "We can't find the heartbeat, so we're going to insert an Internal Fetal Monitor into your baby's scalp, okay?" *Not ideal, but do whatever is necessary to find the heartbeat.* "Abby, we need to do an emergency C-section now. You're hemorrhaging, and the baby's heart rate keeps decelerating." *Absolutely, you're the doctor.*

Into the world came our healthy baby girl—no indication as to why I was hemorrhaging or why her heart rate was decelerating—and it didn't matter one bit because she was perfect. Bring on the anxiety. I didn't sleep the first night: What if her heart rate dropped again? What if she stopped breathing? What if the nurses find out that I'm actually not qualified to be a mom, and they don't let us take her home? Anxiety + Imposter Syndrome = Momposter Syndrome . . . I had it bad, and that ain't good! I would worry obsessively that my anxiety was going to spill onto my babe. I thought she would absorb my negative feelings and grow up to be a never-ending ball of worry, that she would struggle before she even had a chance to start. And then I realized that if I truly believed that, the opposite must also be true.

If I have the power to pass on my anxiety, I also have the power to pass on my happiness and enthusiasm for life.

So, I chose the latter. I focused on showing her my joy. It doesn't mean I never feel anxious in front of her; of course, I do. But it does mean that when those anxious feelings come up, I can take that feeling, acknowledge it, and send it straight out the freaking door.

YOU ARE WORTHY OF RECEIVING HELP

The first week at home was exhausting and wonderful. My mom stayed to help us find our footing in these new roles, and my husband was off work. We were the happiest little bundle of baby-loving humans around. And then we all got sick; seven days into our new baby's life, we all got hit with the worst cold the world had ever seen (or so we thought). How could we let a bug get to our precious babe?! I cried night and day—feelings of mom guilt combined with missing my own mother who had to go home early because of this dang cold. Top it off with what I later found out was postpartum anxiety and depression, and you've got yourself a recipe for a flood of constant tears.

My husband was our rock: grocery shopping, feeding me, cleaning, making sure I got the necessities; he did everything for us. EVERYTHING. And yet, I still couldn't stop crying. I couldn't shake this feeling that someone was going to find out that I didn't know how to be a mother and take Elizabeth away from me. Or, that she knew I didn't know how to be a mother and already resented me for it. I needed help, but the guilt of asking for it was overwhelming. I should be able to get this under control! I'm the organized planner who takes on hundreds of things at once, so I think I can raise a freaking baby! But what it came down to was not feeling worthy of needing help. I had a supportive family, the best husband I could've ever dreamed of, and yet I was still struggling.

There are women out there doing this all on their own, and I felt like my asking for help was taking away from their needs. Not true, by the way. Postpartum anxiety and depression don't discriminate—they can hit anyone at any time, whether you have a village or not. This was a hard lesson to learn, and truthfully one I still revisit regularly. But that's part of growing, right? You don't just check the box—lesson learned, next!—and move on. You have to practice.

Everything you learn, the tools you pick up in life, are stored in your brain, and the more you use them, the easier it is for your brain to find them. After one particularly tough conversation with my husband, we agreed that I should get professional help. I got on a waiting list for the maternal mental health clinic in Vancouver . . . but it was an eight-week wait. That's like eight years in new baby land. So, I found a private counsellor who specialized in postpartum anxiety. Talking to her was like letting light in through the branches of my dark forest. It wasn't even the things she said that lifted me, it was that I could talk to someone who didn't need to offer me their advice but would if I asked. She would hold my baby so I could drink hot tea, or do squats with me because it seemed to be the only thing that kept this sweet babe from crying.

I was learning that although I was doing everything I could to keep this child healthy and happy, I also needed to do the same for myself.

It was not always easy to ask for help. First of all, I didn't even know what to ask for. *Excuse me neighbor, can you hold my crying baby for ten minutes while I take a much-needed shower?* So, I practiced. I wrote down the things I could do for myself even if I only had a few minutes. I asked my husband to hold her so that I could stand up and make dinner. I'm a terrible cook, but I was desperate to get my butt off the couch and contribute something to the household (other than successfully keeping a tiny human alive).

Having vulnerable conversations with my counsellor made it easier to have them with others. I slowly but surely broadened my circle of moms to lean on. I found friends in unexpected places: women from my prenatal yoga class; mom groups on Facebook; friends from the past who'd had babies. One of my unexpected connections was with my high school best friend; she reached out with an offer of essential oils to help Elizabeth with her digestion and potentially ease her crying. That one point of connection has changed our lives, and it made me realize that's all it takes sometimes—one point of connection; one hand reaching out; one mom sharing her story to know that I wasn't the only one feeling this.

GIVE YOURSELF GRACE AND SPACE TO PRACTICE

Life was starting to get back to a new normal; Elizabeth was no longer crying twenty hours a day, and neither was I. My work in the natural health community led to a mindset training program that solidified what we were learning bit by bit as new parents. Through this program, I began to create and connect my vision for our future with the actions and emotions I needed to experience to get there. I started incorporating my essential oils into anchoring those emotions so that they would propel me further in my business, which had a ripple effect that carried over into all parts of my life.

Getting those small wins—with Elizabeth's health, starting a business, connecting with our community—reinforced that I was, in fact, on a path. I didn't know where it was leading, but I had faith that the universe did. I started to see that even in those moments when I didn't know what the outcome was going to be, something was pushing me to take action anyway. And even though it took thirty-six years to build up this trust and confidence in myself to move forward, it was the birth of our rainbow baby that solidified it.

It turns out that when you have a baby, you can plan all you like, but eventually you have to learn to let go and trust your instincts.

I began reflecting on the first three months of Elizabeth's life; it had been hard, beautiful, sad, exciting, and every emotion in between—the paradox of parenthood. I regretted that I had spent so much of it balled up with fear, and I knew I needed to do everything in my power to lessen the weight of postpartum anxiety for others. Thus, *Wellness Creek Co.* was born, a place where I could connect new parents with their own complementary care team, create wellness plans to get them on the other side of darkness, and share my love of what these essential oils had done for our family.

I gained confidence in my skills as a mother and as a partner, and I could feel my strength coming back. This is how I built my own path to wellness—one step at a time. Taking control of the things I could and letting go of the things I couldn't. It became easier to move beyond just surviving the day, and to see the amazing things that were happening all around us. Elizabeth was learning something new every day, and so was I. The greatest lesson of all was in releasing the plan and acknowledging that I have the power to control how I'm feeling, one moment at a time.

ACTIONS TO FEEL BETTER TODAY:

- Make a list of things you can control: taking vitamins; drinking enough water; taking deep breaths. When you feel like you're spinning, run through your list. Choose an action that you can take in that moment to ground yourself.
- Take a few minutes every day to visualize your future: how you want to feel; where you are; who is around you. Focus on the emotion.
- Connect with one person every day. We are community-driven beings by nature, and as such, we crave connection. If you feel like you don't have anyone to connect with, send me a message, even if it's just an emoji. I'll know what you mean, and I'll be right there (virtually of course, that would be weird if I showed up at your house).
- Make a gratitude list: write it out, or say it out loud. Turn it into a song to sing with your babe!
- Take one tiny step toward your vision every day. Incorporate one new habit that moves you closer to your dream. Remember you are on the right path; you just have to keep walking.

Start now, get into the routine of practicing gratitude and building your daily habits one at a time to give yourself back your superpowers, because I know you've got them, mama, you wouldn't be here if you didn't. May you see the joy and light that you carry with you every day. I do, and I can't wait for you to share it with the world.

Chapter Sixteen

Why The *Me* In Mom*Me* Matters

"They say you can't pour from an empty cup, but instead of focusing on pouring, we need to start focusing on filling. Filling ourselves up first so that we're not empty when we give out."

Teresa Sturino Schiavone

TERESA STURINO SCHIAVONE

ig: @sassicreative
sassicreativeco.com

Teresa Sturino Schiavone is an award-winning editor with over fifteen years of experience helping organizations build their brands and tell their stories through roles in marketing, public relations, and communications. After the birth of her daughter, Sienna, in 2015, Teresa decided to leave her corporate life behind. Inspired by her love of writing and her passion for style and design, she began her own consulting boutique *Sassi Creative Co.*, and founded a magazine sharing and celebrating women's stories. She credits her motherhood journey as the inspiration to start pursuing her dreams and live the life she wanted. Teresa resides in Mississauga, Ontario, with her daughter and husband, and hopes that by sharing her story she can inspire other women to do the same.

Why The *Me* In Mom*Me* Matters

MOMME MIND GAMES: MENTAL HEALTH, AND WHY IT MATTERS

I t was a rainy spring night; I remember the sound of the downpour hitting my sister's car. The rain was coming down so hard and so fast, I felt like the water was going to break through the roof. She had taken me to get a coffee, a welcomed break and escape for this semi-new mama. My sister looked at me after she pulled up and parked in my driveway, and even though she hadn't said a word yet, my soul knew something big—something life-changing—was about to happen. My heart understood that my sister knew me better than anyone, and so I looked at her and listened. "What's wrong? Talk to me. What's going on? This isn't you," she said. And then, just like the rain, my tears started streaming down my cheeks, so hard and so fast. I almost couldn't breathe, as if my breath might somehow slow my tears. She leaned over and hugged me and, at that moment, even though I hadn't said a word yet, my soul—my heart—knew that she helped save me.

And then it all came out, the sound of my downpour in the stillness of her car. I replied, "Everything. I'm miserable. I feel lost. I feel alone. I'm the worst mother. I'm so angry all the time. I don't recognize myself. I don't know who I am anymore. I can't fit into any of my clothes. I'm so out of shape. I don't know where I'm going in life. I haven't showered in three days. I don't have a career anymore. I miss my friends. I miss being able to go out whenever I want. Look at me?! I left the house in a dirty shirt and slippers. I should feel grateful. I should be happy. I should feel so lucky. I have a beautiful baby girl, I have all this love around me and so many amazing people who help me. Why? Why do I feel this way?" Exhale. Phew, was I glad that came out. It was as if the sum of the past fourteen months all came out at once.

She looked at me, in her bad-ass half-spiritual goddess, half Superwoman aura, and said these two simple words, "You matter." Followed by a few other important words I'll never forget: "You're worth it. You're amazing. You deserve to live the life you want and be whomever you want to be. Your dreams are important. You still have time to do everything you want to do. Don't let anyone or any bullshit-beliefs you have, stop you from that."

We talked for over an hour, and just as I was saying goodbye, she said, "Before you go to sleep tonight, write a list of who you are as a mom, and who you are as a person. Put down everything you want to be, and everything you want to do. I'll call you tomorrow."

THE ME IN MOM MATTERS

So, there I was . . . After putting my daughter Sienna to sleep, I stared down at the blank page of my journal. The tears started welling up again, but this time it was partly because I knew my sister was going to follow up, and partly because deep down, I knew this was the soul-searching I needed; I started to write. In column one, in all lowercase, I jotted down the word mom. In column two, in all caps, I jotted down the word ME. The more I looked at the words, the more I thought, and the more I thought, the more I got to thinking. I started to remind myself of the woman I used to be before I became a mom—the girl that I worked so hard to become. I said the words out loud "mom," "me." I then said them again. The me in mom mattered.

> *And it was that exact moment, the kind of quint-essential "Hallmark" movie moment where it all made sense, and all the clichés came crashing toward me at once.*

For me to be the best mom, I had to be the best me. How could I possibly pour from an empty cup? How could I teach my daughter to chase her dreams and follow her heart when I wasn't? I have to lead by example. I have to show up. I have to be real, true to myself. I have to believe that I matter—that taking care of myself matters and that what I want matters. Authentically me. Not some "show mom" who tries to be something she's not because she thinks she needs to be someone else.

THE MOMME MASKS WE WEAR

I remember reading about the oxygen mask theory. I was amazed to learn that the reason they remind you to "Put your own mask on first before you help others" is because the concept is counter-intuitive. This couldn't be more true. As women, as mothers, we're natural nurturers and caregivers. Whether it's through conditioning, basic instinct, or both, women tend to carry the brunt of caring and tending to their children, to those they love, to the matters of the home.

As a history minor, I naturally started thinking about the history of women and why we subconsciously and consciously sometimes feel this pressure. This type of acclimatizing and conditioning dates back to ancient times and spans so many different classes, races, and cultures. The one trend is that each type of society had its own set of standards and conventional roles for men and women, which in turn were passed down generationally.

Sadly, even to the present day, women are still sometimes judged and valued based on their status as a wife or mother. Even more disheartening is that some of the shaming and guilt women feel is perpetuated by other women. Topics like whether women want children, or choose to have a career, or even engage in self-care have somehow become a competition. Almost as if one way is better than the other, or one dream has more merit than the other. This couldn't be further from the truth. There are some women who are truly fulfilled by staying home to care for their families. I applaud those women; I support those women, and I value those women. The key to supporting each other is that all the women like me who want, choose, or have to work, are equally applauded, supported, and valued in the same way for following their own truth and living their own way.

The fundamental factor is making choices based on our own set of circumstances, and not based on how we think we should live, or who we should be.

We live in the twenty-first century, and I can't tell you how many times people, most often women, would question and frown at me for going back to work and enrolling Sienna in daycare. I heard everything from, "You're leaving her with strangers?" to "Isn't she too young?" to "Can't your husband support you?" to my personal favorite: "Aren't you afraid she's going to forget you?" Is this even a thing? Last time I checked, I was going to work for eight hours, not to the moon for all of eternity! It's headshaking to think this type of gender bias still exists, which is minor in comparison to the many disturbing inequities and inhuman hardships far too many women still face around the world every day.

MY "NOT SO NORMAL" NORMAL

This got me thinking about my childhood, the roles women (and men) played, and how they shaped me. Having the privilege to grow up in an environment where stereotypical roles were my "not so normal,

normal" isn't lost on me. The women in my life were natural trailblazers, which was not socially celebrated in the era they lived in. I remember my grandmother, Nonna Teresa (my namesake), would recount the stories of her taking three busses to work at a button factory, making minimum wage—which was less than the minimum wage for men—the cruel conditions they worked in, all the labour and "grunt work" they were given while all the men were given positions of power. Then there's my great-aunt, Rita, whose sheer strength and will allowed her to own her own hair salon and small café. Both of these women chose to conquer convention, all while enduring the additional prejudice they faced for being new immigrants.

Skipping a generation, and my mother has her own set of stories. At her first job with a very large company, she was passed up for a promotion on three separate occasions, while her male colleagues advanced. It wasn't until she pointed this inequity out to her manager that she was finally supported and promoted.

I would also never negate all the amazing fathers or male figures who contribute. In fact, when we were younger, we all called my dad "Mr. Mom" because he was always so hands-on, present, and helpful around the house. I mean, come on, even the nickname "Mr. Mom" is steeped in the traditional roots of women. Coming from an Italian background, this was definitely not the typical role men played in the family. And even though our grandfathers contributed to the home more than their relatives or peers, there was still more pressure placed on the women in our family to make sure we were "marriage and mother material."

THE MOMME PANDEMIC PRESSURE COOKER

From the plethora of sacrifices to the barrage of responsibilities and the life-altering changes women have to embrace, adapt to, and navigate through—the constant struggle and juggle is real! Part of this pressure-cooker mentality is propagated by this unrealistic idea that women need to "just handle it." Statistically, during this epidemic, women took on additional responsibility, including things like homeschooling. Whether you're a homemaker, a working-mama, or a superhero single mom, women were now expected to be fully present at their job while also being fully there for their children (which, by the way, we all know includes a bottomless list of snacks, endless amounts of mom-calling, and an unhealthy level of exhaustion, caffeine, alcohol, or all three!). Regardless of the support women received from family or spouses, they still somehow had to manage more while taking and having less for themselves.

We have to look no further than the conditions of the current pandemic to see the challenging imbalance women continuously face.

THE WEIGHT AND WORTH OF MOMS

One of the most common implicit beliefs that women subscribe to is this notion that they should matter less than those they care for. That the needs of others supersede their own. Maybe at times they do, and that's okay, that's life—but they can't all the time, because that's not living. It doesn't matter how old you are or at what stage of the motherhood journey you're in, you need to make time for yourself, to regularly practice self-care, to invest in yourself, to take care of *you*. Whether you're a mom to a newborn or on the other end of the cycle caring for a parent, you still matter. I see this struggle at play with my mother currently as she still works full-time while simultaneously taking care of her ageing mother. As she struggles internally with the guilt of not being able to care for her and potentially putting her into a long-term care facility, I feel the weight of that pressure—and I recognize that conflict all too well. My mom is the most selfless person I know, always helping and giving of herself to others—too much sometimes, which is common for a lot of women.

I remember flipping through so many books when I was pregnant, but, among all the books and internet scrolling, I never came across the importance of taking care of myself, the woman, *after baby*. Women need support so that we don't feel so alone. So that we don't feel like less of a mom for still wanting to live a life outside of diapers and onesies.

We still deserve to dream, even if those dreams change or evolve.

Now, this doesn't mean we negate our responsibilities; it means the exact opposite, in fact. It means we're empowering ourselves and our responsibilities by living by our terms and conditions. Some of you may be reading this, thinking *how is this even possible* (and maybe you even rolled your eyes!). I get it. I've been there. It doesn't mean the same or look the same for everyone. Everyone's wants and needs are different, their own, and theirs to own. For me, at first, it looked like carving out time to exercise, to shower, to put on some makeup, to give myself permission to start believing again. To remind myself that I mattered enough to take care of myself so that, in turn, I can take care of my daughter. To stop hiding behind some preconceived idea that I had to give up my plans or become someone I wasn't. It doesn't happen overnight. Progress over perfection; so I took steps every day. It eventually developed into reading again, journaling, taking some courses, starting a business, and investing in myself. I'm living unapologetically so that I never have to feel bad for feeling good.

MORE THAN A MOM

Motherhood is hard work, period. There is so much pressure to have it all and be it all. Moms are magically supposed to wear as many hats as humanly, and not-so-humanly, possible. Sadly, the stigma and "mommy-guilt" silences a lot of women and prevents them from seeking help when they need it. I've been so fortunate with all the help I receive, but even I hid my true feelings in shame, thinking I was inferior for feeling the way I did. Of course, we love our children and our parents. I love my daughter infinitely, and most importantly, unconditionally—but how can I love her that much when I only occasionally and (most unfortunately) conditionally love myself? For so many years, I tried to convince myself that for me to love her as much as I did, I had to somehow love myself less. I had it backwards. I needed to love the woman I was—the mother of a beautiful miracle baby who was ready to continue her life's journey alongside her daughter, rather than watch her daughter's journey separately from the side. There was a difference. One that I didn't allow myself to entertain because somehow, I felt like I would be less of a mother if my life included more than being a mom.

Who we are and what we want doesn't have to disappear with the diapers in the "diaper genie"! For some, it happens instantly, for others it may take some time, but we need to start honoring the woman within. We need to start recognizing that the *me* in the mom matters enough to care for her, nurture her, and love her. To show the same amount, or more, kindness and compassion that we have for others. They say you can't pour from an empty cup, but instead of focusing on pouring, we need to start focusing on filling. Filling ourselves up first so that we're not empty when we give out. Do the work, grow, challenge yourself to push past your comfort zone, and become the biggest cheerleader for the woman you always wanted to be. Take action, no matter how small.

Whether it's reading a book or journaling or taking up a hobby, try to do something every day that makes you happy.

MOMME MANUAL AND MANTRAS

Looking back, that spring night undoubtedly changed the course of my life, how I looked at myself, and how I viewed motherhood. It would set me on a path of rediscovering who I was and how I wanted to show up for my daughter and ultimately for myself. The journey of motherhood is like the journey of life; "mama's gotta grow" today, tomorrow, and every day—no matter what life throws our way. There is no singular "Momme Manual," you create your own, and it's definitely not a one-size-fits-all approach. There is one mantra that I assumed during the recent pandemic, that I repeated whenever I started to feel like I wasn't enough, or that my needs weren't important, or that my imperfections were the sum of my whole parts. And that was, "The me in momme matters, today, tomorrow, and every day." It may not look the same for you, but make that list, devote time for yourself, for self-care, spend time doing things for you and only you. You deserve it, and my hope is that all of you amazing women see yourself the way others do and always empower the *me* in you!

Chapter Seventeen

Let Them Come. Let Them Be. Let Them Go.

"Healing doesn't happen by fixing the broken; it takes place by rebuilding the **unbroken** within."

Angel Kibble

ANGEL KIBBLE

www.angelempowerment.ca
ig: @angelempowerment | fb: @angelempowerment

Angel Kibble is a mother, author, and Canadian Army Veteran who draws on her life's story, intuition, and passion to inspire, empower, and encourage others to embrace a healthy, fulfilling, and purpose-driven life. Angel is an award-winning, best-selling author and Trauma Informed Certified Coach. She embraces a holistic approach to life's challenges while maintaining a slower pace, and allowing a healthy balance in life while nurturing her soul. Born in Sarnia, Ontario, and spending most of her youth in the Okanagan, Angel now resides with her husband, children, and service dog on beautiful Vancouver Island. Though, not as she envisioned, her journey through life is one of hope, inspiration, and true resilience. Being the warrior she is, Angel will continue to share stories from her soul in future publications.

Let Them Come. Let Them Be. Let Them Go.

As a mother of five beautiful, unique, and precious children, I have been truly blessed and grown in ways I never imagined possible. As my children are transitioning into young adulthood, I can now reflect on lessons learned and my extensive growth in a manner only time and experience affords.

Having been born into severe generational dysfunction, I lived through extensive abuse and adversity. While many cannot rise above the ashes of their past, my pain, protective instincts, and desire for a better life became my driving force. I pivoted and completely changed the trajectory of my life, and I have worked tirelessly at breaking the dysfunction that was my unwanted birthright. As a result, I now live a life filled with beauty, balance, and purpose. While many discover who they are as individuals during adolescence and early adulthood, I found myself, at times, an overwhelmed mother of three exceptional, beautiful children—focused on our survival and personal discovery.

Inexplicable endless love for my children and a fearless maternal protective instinct came naturally and immediately.

I was, and am to this day, a fiercely protective mama bear—though, at times, lost within my pain. I was my children's sole guardian, provider, and protector as circumstances initially took us on a dark, deep downward spiral. Despite my efforts and best intentions, my attempts to protect us were, sometimes, unsuccessful. The many obstacles that hindered my path have, at times, been more than I could manage alone—while the struggles I faced have unintentionally subjected us all to immense pain. I've always invited the excitement of the world into my children's lives so one day they may leave the comfort and protection I provide, and successfully venture into life on their own. I don't know about all you mama bears, but I never had any training, preparation, or the faintest inkling of what it took to be a parent. As a child, abuse of all kinds was the *norm*. I was a child myself, only sixteen, when I first became a mother and started my parenting journey.

I have always enjoyed teaching and seeing the world through my children's innocent and curious eyes as we explored the many wonders of the world together. Despite my troubled upbringing, when I saw my firstborn, I knew that I would fight to ensure that my children would not experience the world I knew. None of my children came with instruction manuals, and no qualifications or licensing was required—pretty much anyone can become a parent. We learn and implement our parenting skills from our parents, upbringings, role models, society, and mostly we learn by trial and error. The world I knew as a child did not prepare me in any way to be a parent. Fortunately, maternal nurturing has always come naturally to me.

My children amaze me every day. I have learned I am just as much their student as their teacher. I appreciate and value each lesson as I continue to learn from them as we all mature and transition into our new stages of life. The more I learned, the more I realized there are so many lessons that lie ahead. While my children may never fully understand the depth and complexity of the love I have for them, I strive every day for them to feel loved, respected, honored, and cherished.

Unsure what our future would hold, and envisioning a beautiful life much like the numerous fairy tales I read to my children, I fully embraced the many challenges of being a single working mother. Eventually, I went on to join the Canadian Armed Forces, where I was blessed to have met and married a like-minded amazing man, and his beautiful children, who I love and cherish as my own. He has been my best friend, confidant, companion, and rock in all life aspects.

Unexpectedly, my career was cut short. My military service left me with severe, permanent, debilitating injuries secondary to physical, moral, and sexual traumas that I experienced while in uniform. This affected our daily lives. Ingrained beliefs and behaviors that once kept me safe, sometimes created unnecessary pain, suffering, and confusion for us all.

Our family has been through or exposed to far more than our fair share of challenges: divorce, dysfunction, addictions, unimaginable abuse, life-altering injuries, abandonment, and poverty. Through it all, I have managed well in certain moments, while at other times, I have fallen apart. Both physically and emotionally, my pain has, and at times still, consumes me. While I cannot control things externally, I have learned to manage my reactions better. My attempts to hide my pain and suffering from my children have been unsuccessful, and sometimes detrimental to us all. I find this to be a common characteristic among many mothers and caretakers.

Losing myself affected my ability to be present and fully engaged with myself, others, and, most notably, my children.

All children are deserving of and thrive amongst safety, stability, nurturing, solid guidance, and unconditional love. Being honest with myself and loved ones while facing my many obstacles head-on releases me from my internal turmoil, and protects my children from unintended baggage that is not theirs to carry. I have had much baggage thrown at me by many, and I have often wondered how I ever survived. Yet, I eventually learned to thrive despite adversity. We, as humans, are hardwired to endure much, and we are far more resilient than we realize. If we don't overcome the challenges we face, they continue to present themselves in multiple ways until we can learn from and conquer them. I consistently return to the drawing board, assessing and reassessing the many lessons learned as I move toward my next best step for myself and my family.

Like a mama bear, keeping my cubs healthy and safe requires me to keep myself strong and balanced, both physically and mentally, in all pillars of life. Having a sense of self-love, acceptance, belonging, and safety has granted me the ability to be better equipped to connect with myself, my children, and society as a whole. I eventually realized that I was not broken; instead, I required restructuring and needed to focus on myself. Many of us, much like bears, wander through life driven by survival instincts—rather than being mindfully present—without understanding the toll it takes. While some of us come from peaceful uninhabited forests, others, such as myself, had their environments destroyed numerous times. Often, I had to find and rebuild safe new surroundings. Sadly, many cannot do this and find themselves trapped within dysfunction. Life is ever-evolving, and unlike bears, we as human beings can change our beliefs, behaviors, environments, and the trajectory of our individual lives. If we hold on to belief patterns that no longer serve us, we become trapped in unhealthy behaviors and old habits, which keep us locked in unhealthy relationships and environments. Shifting our beliefs naturally changes our behaviors, and opens us to new ways of living—far more incredible than any fairy tale.

Despite my strength and resilience, I could not control the numerous internal and external hardships which left me fighting for my life while raising a family. Despite my best efforts, I was not initially equipped to keep balanced and safe from the chaos and traumas I endured. However, I knew that I needed to continue breaking the cycle for myself and my family. I had to limit, and even end, toxic relationships with those who remain stuck in their dysfunction or unhealthy lives—all as part of pivoting in new and healthy directions in my own life. I will not pretend that this was easy to do. I always keep a space in my heart for those I cannot hold close, as I continue to maintain and enforce healthy boundaries in all areas of life. Trying to grow and blossom was all but impossible in those unhealthy relationships and dangerous environments.

I knew I needed to be a strong, steady, well-balanced presence for both myself and my family.

The excellent news, mama bears, is that as hard as it was, this has allowed me to bloom and discover a whole new world; the one that I had always imagined was out there. Though it was not easy and took me many years to achieve—separating from the environment and people who are not in the same place of personal growth and reinvention has been confusing, painful, and overwhelming—it has also brought me safety, clarity, and much-needed fulfillment. I continue to surround myself with genuinely wonderful, amazing friends, family, and relationships—which I am beyond grateful for every day.

My continued efforts to break the cycle of generational dysfunction have set a positive and healthy example for my children, despite my imperfections. Healing our traumas and wounds is a lifelong commitment that takes endless energy and effort as we peel back each individual layer. Peeling back the layers has gotten messy, to put it mildly. It has often been more than I could manage alone. I have found and continue to surround myself with a solid support system that includes family, friends, respected persons, professionals, community support, and continuous education. My network provides my family and me with strength and safety when I cannot muster it independently. Previously, my self-care was limited or non-existent as I was in survival mode. Prioritizing my children's well-being over my own was my only choice, as I didn't have the energy for both. Putting myself first required me to do concentrated, intensely personal work, not once, twice, or a handful of times—but consistently and mindfully every day. Even now, I still find myself getting caught in old patterns. However, I can now acknowledge it and do the needed course correction to get back on track.

Honoring and respecting where I am in my journey continues to serve me well. Breaking the cycles that once ruled my life allows me to discover myself and reflect on who I have become. I learned that living a happy, fulfilled life isn't a destination with an arrival date; instead, it means caring for myself and nurturing my individual wants and needs—while chasing my dreams and living a life of purpose. This belief system allows me to live a happy, fulfilled life every day to be mindfully present for myself and my children. I take an interest in and encourage their individual passions and dreams, while modelling and prioritizing my own. This is important, especially as western society tends to be disconnected, fast-paced, and chaotically unbalanced. I learned to ignore unhealthy societal norms and honor where we are individually in life, as we are all truly unique and grow at different rates. As humans, I believe we all are here to live our own individual experiences.

It is never too late to return to ourselves if we lose our way.

Self-care isn't a checklist or a one-size-fits-all solution; instead, we must build a consistent and healthy way of life for ourselves and our families by showing up mindfully each moment of every day. I am not suggesting we should in any way neglect our children; instead, if we don't prioritize ourselves and lead by example, we will never be able to show up for our children fully. They really do learn what they live and see. I learned the hard way that our bodies and brains remain instinctually hardwired, despite immense evolution. We are not designed to live in constant survival mode. If we do, our physical and psychological health will eventually fail. I have experienced this in several ways, including anxiety, depression, post-traumatic stress disorder (PTSD), various chronic pain disorders, heart issues, irregular blood pressure, chronic fatigue, complex regional pain syndrome (CRPS), and complete dorsal vagal nerve shut down. The list is extensive and has nearly cost me my life. A few resources I highly recommend include: *The Polyvagal Theory* by a leading neuroscientist, Stephen W. Porges; *The Body Keeps the Score* by Bessel Van Der Kolk, M.D., Director of Psychiatry at Boston University School of Medicine; and *When the Body Says No, The Cost of Hidden Stress* by Gabor Mate, M.D., a renowned speaker and best-selling author.

Healing our traumas affords us the ability to break free from cages that once held us captive. Doing so allows us to create a safe, peaceful environment crucial to thriving rather than just surviving. Healing and growth are lifelong commitments that are as complex and individual as each of us. At times, it can seem impossible; however, it is ever so rewarding and opens us to be present for ourselves and our children. Like a mama bear, I am fiercely protective, yet, unlike bears, I have learned to care for myself and my cubs proactively—rather than reactively—by controlling and changing my environment. My children know their mama bear is always nearby, watching over them as they venture into adulthood and learn from their own successes and failures. It has taken me years to realize that I am responsible *to* myself, children and others; however, I am only responsible *for* myself.

When I feel unbalanced or that the world's weight is upon my shoulders, I know it is a warning that I need to pause, step back, and use my *tools*, including breath work, basic grounding, meditation, and yoga, to assess my next best move. I have also learned to sit with my emotional discomfort, as this is where I learn, grow, and connect with my inner child and authentic self. Sitting with myself in a safe place allows the time and space I need to continue healing. Being compassionate with myself, allowing my emotions to run free, and labelling them as they arise has allowed immense release, understanding, and ultimately growth. We have but one life and get to choose each day how to live it—so make it beautiful.

Reconnecting with myself has been the greatest gift I could give to my children.

I have learned to love myself completely, forgive my wrongdoings, and let go of the shame and blame I once carried. Our thoughts control our emotions and actions—mindfully altering our thoughts can change our beliefs and behaviors. It's crucial that we, along with our children, get the best version of ourselves every day. Life has a way of sneaking up and catching us off guard. To remain balanced individually and as parents, we need to ride the tides of time mindfully. Being at one with myself allows me to hold the space required for myself, my children, loved ones, and ultimately, you—reading my words.

Tell your children you love them; watch over them when they stray, and let them know you will always be their greatest fan and forever supporter. Make sure they *feel* your love, rather than just hear it in the words you say. Lead by example and show them that the most crucial person is oneself—knowing it is a beautiful journey when we embrace the ebb and flow of it all.

Never give up.

Anything is possible if you always make the next best move for yourself your family. Healing doesn't happen by fixing the broken; it takes place by rebuilding the *unbroken* within. Every emotion, circumstance, and situation is temporary and transient. Let them come. Let them be. Let them go.

Chapter Eighteen

Perfectly Grateful

"Gratitude is a great foil for perfectionism;
where you are always looking for what's wrong
in perfectionism, in gratitude, you're looking
for what's working well."

Sonia Dong

SONIA DONG

web: www.henkaa.com
ig: @soniadong | fb: @sidekicksonia
li: @soniadong

Sonia is an earth-loving mama of two girls who runs *Henkaa*, a socially impactful Toronto clothing brand. Through *Henkaa*, she is creating a fashion revolution where one-time-use special occasion dresses and tops become a thing of the past, and where body-positive, size-inclusive clothing that journeys with women and girls through all seasons of life becomes the norm—rather than the exception. Prior to joining *Henkaa*, Sonia worked in the environmental non-profit field, focused on program development for students, professional development, and diversity and inclusion. She has held positions on several Boards of Directors for local community organizations, and is currently a Donor Advisor to the *Joanna Duong Chang Memorial Foundation*.

Perfectly Grateful

Even before I became a mom, I struggled with perfectionism. I didn't identify it as perfectionism though, I just knew that I liked things to be a certain way, and I liked being in control. Attempting to live up to all those baby books I read, to execute what I learned from other moms and classes I attended, left me feeling like a failure whenever something didn't work out. I felt defeated and frustrated, always striving to figure out this thing called *mom-hood*, and asking myself:

Why can't I get this right for once?

Right, wrong, perfect, imperfect, good enough, not good enough. While I was growing up, and as a new mom, it really was that black and white for me. There was no in-between, and the concept of constructive criticism was very challenging for me to grasp. I remember crying in grade school when a teacher said that my book report was overall very good, and there were some things she suggested to make it even better the next time. All I heard was: "You suck." Growing up in an immigrant Asian household, there were questions like, "You got 98% on your test, what happened to the other 2%?" I don't blame my parents. As an adult, I can read between the lines: "Always try your best. The higher your grades, the more opportunities you'll have, starting with the opportunity to go to university, which we never had. And that means you'll have a shot at a better job that pays well and provides you with stability, so you won't have to struggle like we did." But as a child, I could not interpret the 2% gap in my test grades—all I knew was they wanted me to be perfect, to get that perfect grade.

As a new mom, other moms and my husband were telling me, "There's no perfect." "Don't listen to those judge-y people." "No one knows what they're doing, we're all learning as we go." But it still took me more than a few years to finally realize that who I was looking for was staring back at me in the mirror. I was already a great mom, but I was also the most judgmental and most fierce critic of myself. I needed to stop beating myself up, stop listening to the negativity in my head, and turn my inner critic into my best cheerleader—my biggest fan. I needed her to remind me that I was doing my best and that when things don't work out, to "let it go" (as *Frozen's* Elsa would say) and move on.

When I had my kids, it was like staring into my own eyes. The things that bugged me the most about my kids' behavior were often the things that I saw as flawed in myself and would end up saying, "I don't like how she's acting. I'm totally messing up as a mom! But wait. She's actually acting like *me*, and that's even more annoying!" This is another area where I think, *Wow, I really am not perfect at all*—and there is so much I still need to do! My kids see me, and they act like me. They also have incredible connectedness to me. Once, my husband and I were arguing, and I was sad, about to cry. My daughter took one look at me and went to get tissues. She wasn't even two years old yet.

So, being my own best friend is taking time.

Building a healthy relationship with myself, learning about me, and doing what is best for me—while also being a compassionate and loving mom and partner—is a journey with its own ups and downs. I still find myself in that perfection-control loop, and it crops up not just in my relationship with myself but in other areas of my life.

Let's take my daughters, for instance: They have this self-awareness that makes them fearful of doing something wrong or not perfectly. They've even stopped themselves from trying for fear of messing things up. One daughter even scribbles out or erases drawings she's made when it doesn't come out the way she envisioned because she doesn't want people to see how it looks. Does this sound extreme?

Maybe not.

When I reflect on this and my own experience, I see how I do something very similar. I think about my own fear, for instance, in writing this chapter. I feel like I'm being vulnerable by putting myself out there, and what that means to me is everyone will see how imperfect I really am. Just like my child who is hiding her artwork by scratching it out, I've been hiding by leaving words off the page, by keeping it in my head—so no one else can see.

I get why my daughter wants to scratch out her drawings—it's because she also feels vulnerable, that maybe she will be judged as imperfect, too. Words really do matter, and I try to refrain as much as possible from imparting that fear of imperfection onto them. In this, I am also imperfect, and that's okay. There's no use beating myself up about it—I need to model the behavior that I want my kids to exhibit, too. I want both of my daughters to see mistakes and things that don't work out the way they wanted them to the first time, to be seen as opportunities for growth—and that I'll be there to support them. To ingrain into them that their "best" is different each day, depending on what else is going on in their lives that is not in their immediate control. I want them to know that they shouldn't dwell on what others think of them—the most important thing is what they think of themselves. This is what I try to tell them, but really, it's as much for me as it is for them.

Each time I'm teaching them and guiding them,
I'm also teaching and guiding myself.

Perfectionism and control show up a lot in my relationship with my husband as well. The relationship we had pre-kids became so much more challenging when we were focused on raising our tiny humans, being sleep deprived, and not having enough time together or alone. I started feeling resentful and also felt like he wasn't seeing, hearing, or listening to me. We had tiffs about the smallest things that blew up into full-blown arguments, with no resolution on either side. Then, we'd get tired and go to sleep, say "forget about it" (but really, it was just a temporary pause), and the cycle would repeat itself again when we were stressed—which was often. It was exhausting, and it seemed like there was no end in sight. I learned in a mommy class that happiness between couples drops after having kids—not exactly a shining testimonial for those wanting to have kids at some point—and I believed it. But what I also believed was there must be a way to get out of the funk. There must be something to switch up our narrative, to pivot our relationship in a different direction.

And so I went on a hunt—to learn about happiness in a relationship. What worked and what continues to work is a gratitude practice. We were having a hard time communicating with each other face to face— somehow, we just kept saying the wrong things to each other, or we would say things we didn't mean, or say things that were just plain mean! We started writing to each other (in a private blog shared between us), to express our frustrations, and always ended with one or more things we appreciated about the other person.

Through this process, I discovered that I was taking him for grant-ed—that I'd stopped saying thank you and good morning and that my attitude was very negative.

The Little Things
I'm always talking about how the little things mean so much to me and I realized that I haven't been grateful, or take for granted many of those little things you already do, like fill the car tires up with air so I don't have to! That's really only one of many. I need to take a step back sometimes and rec-ognize all that is being done rather than what is not.

The writing allowed both of us to process our emotions and thoughts to be more rational about what was going on, and it started becoming easier to tell each other what we were grateful for in each other, too. And then, slowly, our icy relationship became warmer again.

Healing
It scares me so much that things may not get better. I look at how things are, and think, how could our relationship be so broken? What could we, could I, have done differently? But then, there's no use looking at the past and getting upset about it, we just have to learn from it and look forward. And I do believe that we are on our way to healing ourselves. It will be challenging and sometimes we might want to give up. We will get there. Slowly but surely, we will heal.

If someone were to ask me how we got through those hazy, sleepless nights where we were literally pulling our hair out (both kids were not good sleepers), and then getting into fights, I'd tell them that's what saved our marriage—and that's what saved me from my constant despair.

You're A Great Dad
Don't be so hard on yourself. You're a great dad, and don't let anyone out there (including me) cause you to think otherwise. You think you don't have enough love, or kindness, or patience, or ability, but you are there for them and are more to them every single day. You find it difficult, but who doesn't? If someone says everything is peaches and cream all the time, they're either delusional or they're not actually there when the s&%@ is hitting the fan. No one is perfect, and no one has all the answers. We can only do our best, and I know that you are trying. That's what we say to Arya—try hard, work hard, don't give up, don't say "I can't," because you can, we can, we can be like the little engine that could.

I heard the saying "What you focus on grows" for the first time during this period, and it's true. As we focused on the positive aspects of each other and our relationship, we found more to appreciate and more to love.

We were able to discuss more difficult and frustrating topics face-to-face, without the heat of the moment catching on fire, and for us to listen and/or problem-solve together more easily. Gratitude is a great foil for perfectionism—where you are always looking for what's wrong in perfectionism, in gratitude, you're looking for what's working well.

The writing was also cathartic; even if my husband hadn't read my messages or written back, it still helped me so very much to get it out of me. It gave me the chance to be alone, to reflect on my thoughts too—a valuable thing to have when you're a mom. I take responsibility for that, for carving that time out, listening to myself, and being a good friend to myself. Because as a mom, if I don't prioritize me to be the best that I can be—which includes accepting my failures and mistakes with grace and learning from them instead of being upset—I won't be able to help my kids be the best they can be, either.

Before I had kids, I didn't think I was effective at self-improvement.

Our attitude of gratitude continues to be a theme in the family. With the girls, I'll ask them on walks or before bedtime about what they're grateful for or the thing they most loved about their day. Often they'll say things like ice cream or recess, or their many stuffies, and we'll have a laugh—and they also get to hear from me (and their dad) what or who we are grateful for, too. I hope that by saying these things before bedtime, it gives them some warm fuzzies and sends them off to sleep in good spirits. It's that focus again on something positive and helping them to build that practice, so they focus on what's going well—not on what's perceived as bad, wrong, or imperfect about their lives.

In the world we live in today, with the pandemic and the uncertainties that exist, it's been a real blessing to have this gratitude practice established. March of 2020, we had our vacation plans set up for April, day camps signed up for the summer, cottage trips and camping trips already organized. Then everything changed. Trying to create a new routine for the kids at home, as all moms reading this know, was not easy. I cherished having my husband at home and not traveling for work anymore, and loved not needing to drop off and pick up the kids every day from school. As an extreme introvert, I was happy to be at home and live a quieter life, though, at times, I have to admit I missed having the whole house to myself during the day to work alone! Who knew that having three extra people around 24/7 (even if they weren't in the same room with me all the time) would drain my energy so much? I was also despairing over an ailing business that was hard-hit by the closures, and didn't want my family to see me crying every single day.

Returning to my gratitude practice and to journaling (this time on paper) helped to ground me and build up my energy resources. There were larger forces at work which I could not control and should not try to control. And there were people at home who I could lean on, love, and be loved by—who I was so grateful for. Having gratitude and journaling practices in my "mom toolkit" really gave me a chance to do the self-care I needed, so I could be there for my family.

There's still yelling, bickering, whining, crying, and arguing between all of us—and that's okay—because there's also a lot of laughing, dancing, hugging, and smiles. We're learning together to be grateful, to know what makes us happy as individuals, and how to help others be happy and let go of perfection.

Chapter Nineteen

The Divine Path of Becoming

"Conscious expansion is the loving
awareness that one is continually giving birth to a
new version of self, thus, allowing the eternalness
of who one really is—joyfully."

Tamara Trotman

TAMARA TROTMAN

www.tamaratrotman.com
ig: @tamaratrotman | @jaredandthesacredemerald

fb: @/tamaratrotmancoaching

li: Tamara Trotman | t: @TamaraTrotman
goodreads: Tamara Trotman

Tamara Trotman, a Conscious Entrepreneur, is a catalyst for alignment, and a perpetuator of well-being through writing, teaching, and coaching. Tamara's high vibes and uplifting spirit has inspired her clients for over fifteen years. Living her blessed life in Woodbridge, Ontario, Canada, Tamara resides with her two beautiful kids, Maia and Evan, and amazing husband, Ray. Tamara, a divine soul who loves travelling to exotic new places, nature hikes, and the ocean; follows divine guidance to achieve her greatest potential while joyfully guiding others to do the same.

The Divine Path of Becoming

Imagine standing atop a mountain overlooking a vast valley, abundant in nature of all kinds. The sun shines brilliantly through a mist of white clouds, as they lay effortlessly across a soft blue sky. Sounds of birds chirping in the distance excite and delight. Feeling invincible is enlivened within by the limitlessness which lay ahead. Love, appreciation, a feeling of oneness, and immeasurable peace dominate in what feels like a non-physical hug. Bliss, intoxicatingly savored, until a powerful voice emanates the words:

"Precious One, you have decided to walk this new phase of your experience in physicality, and with great excitement, remind you of some things. As you know, you are pure, positive, powerful energy known as consciousness. Consciousness that is infinite, eternal, and all-knowing. You embody this divine essence, and will desire to authentically express yourself as you walk this physical path of connection; joyously being, doing, and having all that feels true for you. As you mix it up in this physical world, it is your intention to create new experiences not yet lived, and not live what has already been lived. Think of life as a canvas, and you the artist, making deliberate strokes moment by moment into what becomes your masterpiece—much like what you see before you."

Freedom flows like the river below.

"Precious One, within this abundant life, delicious diversity exists for your clarity—for you to choose. It is in this variety that you will know what is truly preferred, giving birth to a new ever-expansive version of yourself, simultaneously allowing for an exhilarating ride."

"Yes, Source, it is my greatest intention to walk in wholeness as I confidently navigate each new experience along my path. It is my desire to appreciate the value of all of it, for it's giving birth to not only new dreams, but the greatest versions of myself."

"And so it is."

THE PHYSICAL EXPERIENCE

With new eyes, a fresh perspective, and unbridled excitement, this physical journey unfolds. Great curiosity, enthusiasm, and joy dominate as new experiences come. A continuous discovery of self fuels all desire to know more. Sheer exhilaration is at an all-time high, as brilliant visions dance like butterflies in the wind. Giggles of laughter fill the air, and feelings of invincibility emanate with such knowing; new experiences are confidently explored. In this form, I am learning to be and express myself in such a melodic, creative way, an unending wave of ease, and rapturous joy flows through me. The perfection with which these moments unfold are so brilliant, that what is referred to as "time" slows, as if not to exist at all.

You are not destined for greatness. You are greatness expressing itself.

As time passes, the influence of others grows stronger, and the inner connection once felt and known grows quieter and quieter. Greater importance is placed on the values and beliefs of others, rather than core intentions set forth by self. An analogy best suited here is that of a hiker. A newborn in its wholeness and perfection, knowing all it knows full of truth and its own intention, is given a hypothetical "backpack." Parents, family, friends, community, and culture all place thoughts, beliefs, values, perceptions, and expectations into this bag, in hopes of creating a "successful being."

As a result, this child inherits a bag full of things that are not a match to who this being really is, thus lured from their own truth, guidance, and knowing for what is wanted—at least for a little while. Things like playing small, overachieving to prove worthiness and value, and sacrificing true happiness to please others. All of these things led to a frantic rummage through my backpack to find relief, quickly realizing the contents inside were only meant for survival and not thriving. What I was ultimately seeking was confidence, clarity, security, and true happiness in each new place I stood.

I, in these unfamiliar places, found myself in several temporary moments of disconnection, or what society terms depression. Each experience gave greater clarity to what was wanted: stop the pain and flow well-being. Each time, gaining powerful awareness to replace what wasn't working with what was. I finally made a choice. To expand joyfully, not in struggle. Light began to penetrate the dark more and more. I now know the difference between the light and the dark, because of these blessed experiences.

There is infinite wisdom within you.

As life continues to unfold, each experience provides opportunities to evolve into who I really am, as I release more contents of the "backpack." Things like: repressing my true brilliance, caring what others think, and doubting my abilities. All of this, I've come to learn, created more resistance—when what I was ultimately seeking was inner peace through completely letting go.

A new desire is born within me to truly know self—who I really was, my purpose, and how to stand authentically in my own power. So, I began to consciously ask myself the following questions: What is my truest intention for being here? Who do I want to be? How do I want to show up in the world? What do I value? What am I a perpetuator of in life and work? The answers began to flow.

Don't do what everyone else is doing,
do what no one else is.

Inspiration to spend time in stillness, focusing on breath, to quiet an overactive mind calls more and more. A steady practice of meditation deepens and a connection to Higher Self and Source is achieved. A powerful new perspective about self is revealed. Through this experience, I have come to understand that I, we, everything emits a frequency. Thoughts one thinks invoke emotions, which influence vibration—high or low. Peaceful moments in stillness allows for non-thought, and a releasing of resistance, which allows vibration to rise and momentum to flow. When this happens, a blending of vibrations with the Divine / God / Source-Self and Physical-Self is accomplished. For example, one summer morning, I sat outside to meditate and asked, "Who am I really? What do you feel for me?" I began to breathe and focus on the sounds of my air conditioner, when I received a vision of myself levitating with powerful beams of light emanating from my extremities—and strong waves of love and appreciation flowed as I heard, "You are love, you are joy, you are infinite, eternal, whole, worthy, and brilliant. This is who you really are."

Tears of worthiness caressed my cheeks for I saw myself in a whole new light for the very first time. It felt pure, powerful, and unconditional. A powerful message—this is not just who I am, but who WE ALL ARE. We can access the "Source within" anytime for guidance, support, and upliftment. Wholeness and worthiness is our birthright. Brokenness, imperfection, and limitedness, I now understand, simply do not exist. It is a false belief perpetuated by many, and of benefit to no one.

It is what you believe that will determine your
enjoyment on this journey.

Through the living of life and powerful divine guidance, a magical unfolding of greater clarity led to a path of many books on personal development, attending the John Maxwell Life Coach Certification Course, and hiring a Life Coach who joyously contributed to my becoming. I felt carefree like a child, skipping along my path, eager for what was coming next. New insights, aha moments, and breakthroughs filled my experience in surprising ways. I was learning to love myself unconditionally, and therefore, stop the struggle and sacrifice. I was becoming who I was truly born to be, and felt the power of standing in my own authentic truth . . . finally.

It's time to shine your light.

One morning in meditation, I felt the usual movement of energy through my body when I heard, "You are going to write a book teaching children how to journey within to love themselves and trust their own inner guidance." It was said with such knowing that I dared-not say no. That evening I was so eager to get started that I sat at my laptop. I took several deep breaths, placed my fingers on the keyboard, and the words began to flow. I repeated this effortless process each night after my kids went to bed, and within six months, finished the manuscript of my first children's book, *Jared and the Sacred Emerald*. I was thrilled. The realization of becoming an author was born.

Follow the path that lights you up the most.

USING THOUGHTS AND EMOTIONS AS POWERFUL GUIDANCE

Through the teachings of deliberate creation by Esther and Jerry Hicks, and my own guidance, I clearly understand just how powerful our thoughts really are. Did you know that if you focus on a thought long enough, like a minute and twenty seconds, it becomes a belief, perspective, and expectation? Not only that, but it evokes emotion, and as a result becomes part of our vibration. Everything around us responds to the vibration we offer. Wow!

From where I now stand, I realize I am responsible for my own experience. I re-examine the contents of the "backpack," and clearly see that the limiting thoughts and beliefs I held were inherited from others, and not my own. This explains my moments of disallowing (depression) of my own power, however, when I received thoughts, ideas, urges, and impulses from Source—and followed through—things changed dramatically. Wonderful things were happening because of what I consciously chose for myself. I was moving joyfully beyond what I thought possible. I was letting go to the point where I no longer needed validation, approval, or permission from others. Greater importance was placed on what I, my Soul, and Source thought and felt about what I was doing. Daily meditation deepened my relationship, and by following all guidance, led to a powerful shift. I was moving more from outer influences, to inner. This relationship now dominates—and by being deliberate in my thoughts and emotions, I raised my vibration higher. I, for the first time, experienced alignment and found myself in wholeness. I joyously released "the backpack", and I love the woman smiling back at me in the mirror.

A technique I use to achieve alignment on any subject is to write positive feeling statements that feel true for me. For example: becoming an entrepreneur *feels fun; I love the freedom of it; I love that I get to choose; I love inspiring conversations with others that expands their minds; I love watching others move in the direction of who they really are.* This is done until an emotional upward shift is experienced. When this is accomplished, one feels excited, exhilarated, eager, happy, and inspired. The more consistent you become in your alignment, the better you feel about who you are, where you are, and where you're headed.

My world is changing because I am changing.

Negative emotion simply means being focused in a way that one's Higher Self isn't. For example, expecting things won't be easy as an entrepreneur, when your Higher Self *knows* things will unfold easily when you allow; or being mad at yourself for not being where you "think" you should be, when your Soul is saying where you are is perfect. It's in the development of this relationship that you can see the variance and adjust thoughts and perceptions that feel better. By doing this consistently, you will raise your vibration, and your ability to receive guidance becomes clearer. In alignment, you feel *so* good because you are connected to *all* of you. This is what "wholeness" is.

The only project you have in this life is you.

THE POWER OF A FOCUSED MIND

The more I quiet my mind and tune myself to the "*Source*" within, the more the outside world becomes irrelevant. When the pandemic occurred, I immediately asked myself what I truly wanted. Vibrant well-being. I visualized adventure, fun, and laughter. I then asked what vibrant well-being felt like. It feels energetic, vital, alive, and exhilarating. I was unwavering in my focus and repeated this all day, every day. The most surprising things began to happen. More experiences like it happened. I would be inspired to work out, and observe streets full of others reflecting vibrant well-being! So in practicing thoughts of what I truly wanted, I aligned with both Source and my true intention to thrive. Powerful . . .

NEGATIVE EXPERIENCES ASSIST IN OUR EXPANSION

There are many circumstances that exist in life that are out of our control, but we do have control over how we feel, and what we focus upon. Based on this experience, I moved beyond what I have done before simply because I cared about how I felt, and my alignment with Higher Self, which led to thriving. True satisfaction was felt by moving in the direction of what I wanted, and I experienced it as a result.

CONSCIOUSLY EXPANDING BEYOND

It is in seeing yourself as spirit in the physical, co-creating with divine power, that conscious awareness is born. It is in allowing life to unfold and consciously following paths that thrill, and by focusing joyfully on them leads to fulfillment and greater expansion. Let's take motherhood for example: It is in the observation of small beings, the visions of ten beautiful toes and an adorable little nose delight, and immense feelings of love that flow at the prospect of holding something so precious and small. Daydreams of giggles fill the mind as one imagines story time, and playful pillow fights. It's these thoughts and powerful emotions that new materializes. Once in this new place, new challenges give birth to more which leads to greater expansion. Instead of being upset with these challenges, one is aware that it is all part of the process, which gives birth to a deeper understanding of self. It is this new place where one is to level up as one realizes current thoughts, beliefs, perceptions, and expectations no longer serve. Belief: Having a baby is easy because all they do is eat and sleep. Situation: What do you mean he has colic and will cry for the next four months??

Truth is, unwanted experiences out of our control happen—but, if you focus on what you truly want with unwavering trust and faith, it will materialize. Visions of a peaceful baby who thrived caressed my thoughts. I focused upon it until answers and solutions were quickly discovered, and with great timing, resolved my son's colic in a week. New belief: Wow! I'm a powerful woman.

Mother's instinct is your divine guidance.

Answers and solutions are ideas received from your Evolved Self. By developing your relationship with Higher Self and Source, one sees things through a compassionate lens for self and others. Annoyance is replaced with appreciation and joy, for one knows more is coming—and more importantly, the "*more*" that is You, is coming, too. It's for these reasons expansion is inevitable, and embracing it for what it is makes for a much smoother journey.

Oftentimes, we observe negative situations and complain, engage in negative conversations to justify where we are, or blame others. This is resistance and makes the journey harder, which is why people feel the need to make growth happen—as opposed to allowing the inevitable to unfold, naturally.

As this chapter demonstrates, *you* are the gift, and self-mastery is the journey. Life is simply helping you to focus yourself into the whole of who you are, in order to live an extraordinarily full life. Through acceptance comes realization that Mama is evolving into the beautiful, blessed being she was truly born to be.

Epilogue

Dearest Mama,

It is our great hope you will continue to grow wherever you're planted. May you rise amidst the storm and be an inspiration to other mamas who experience similar situations, too. We appreciate you being here and are grateful to share our pearls of wisdom with you, from the depths of our being, Thank You. We wish to leave you with a few thoughts as you continue along your journey through motherhood.

Only you know what is best for you and your child(ren). Pay attention to the cues; there are signs all around you, and you're never far from breaking through to the next milestone. As the days, months, and years grow by, please know that you are safe, secure, and supported by Mother Earth, Father Sky, Sister Sun, Brother Moon, and the Universe in its entirety—even in the most challenging times. You carry innate power within you.

*A woman's intuition is never wrong, and a
mother's intuition is increasingly strong.*

We survived our hardest days so far, and we will continue to navigate through any uncharted waters as time progresses. Let us all focus on expanding our consciousness, raising our vibrations, and coming together to heal ourselves, each other, and Mother Gaia, too. The world needs divine love from the feminine now more than ever before. Women, especially mothers, bear the gift of nurturing nature like no other.

You have the power to break the cycle of whatever patterns you refuse to repeat. If you're feeling called to change or grow in a different direction, please honor that. Even though what works for some may not work for all, we support and honor you in your efforts to do and be better for you and your family. It takes a super-woman to mother in any capacity, and that itself is worth acknowledging and celebrating. If you ever question what to do next, remember:

*The future of our children depends on the
actions we take today.*

Do what feels best in your heart, Mama. As long as you lead with love, there is no right or wrong way to "mother". Of all the parenting advice out there, love is at the core, and that's the most important tip of all. Everything else you choose to instill in your children is a bonus, so rest assured you've *got* this, beautiful Mama! No matter what happens, you are doing well by your babes as long as there is love.

May you continue to grow as you adapt to change, shift lifestyles, pivot in pandemic times, and embrace the new "normal" in the ebbs and flows that come your way. We are here for you as a supportive community, and you are welcome to connect with us any time! We're happy to spread love to our fellow mamas and be of service to you however we can.

Here's a little bonus we wish to share with you. It is a daily ritual that is beneficial for adults and especially children—and it takes less than two minutes to do, anytime, anywhere:

"The Mama Gaia Game"

- BY KRYSTA LEE

Begin the day intentionally by taking a conscious moment to express one or more declarations represented in each letter of the word "Gaia," as listed below. This is a basic way to get familiar with positive self-talk, and it is enhanced by speaking aloud and incorporating body movement.

It's a great practice to do with children (during cuddles before rising is lovely!), yet it's just as effective to practice individually, and on the go. It's never too soon or too late to implement this highly effective and impactful practice into your daily rituals. Experiment with modifying your statements as you grow, have fun with it, and enjoy!*

G—is for Gratitude. What are you grateful for today?
A—is for Affirmation. What positive declaration(s) do you affirm for yourself?
I—is for Intention. What is your intention(s) for the day?
A—is for Action. What action step(s) will you take to make the day great?

*Bonus points if you finish your day with "The Mama Gaia Game" too. Grow Team, Grow!

With love, light, and blessings,
-Krysta Lee xox

Acknowledgments

"Thank you for trusting in our circus, Leo and Darcy; together we grow as we find the path that works for our family. Welcome to our circus, C.S."

-Sally Lovelock

"Thank you to my mentors, Linda Casselman of Shield Warriors, and Kimberly Hutt of Souly Reconnected, for inspiring me to seek my truth. Thank you to the team at Golden Brick Road Publishing, for inspiring me to speak my truth."

-Stephanie Barkley-Bequette

"To my babies: Samantha, Liliana, and Marcus who give me strength and bring me joy! My mamma; my papa up in heaven; my sisters, M.M. and girlfriends who have picked me up off the floor one too many times; and of course F.C. and D.T.R. Thank you. ♥"

-Pina Crispo

"Thank you Sara, Ashley, Vanessa, Claudia, Wendy, Marie, Mary, Briana, Hill, Angie, Sue, Jennifer, Anjana, Shadow."

-Whitney Stout

"Thank you to my daughter, Catherine and my sons, Bradlee, Wesley, and Stanley—you make me proud each and every day. To my love and best friend, Bernie, for always supporting me and always being the best."

-Leanne Sigrist

"Thank you to all the souls out there stripping away the armor, and showing up for themselves in all of their humanness. I see you and I love you. And of course, thank you to my soul sister, Krysta, for holding the space for me to share this depth of me."

-Elizabeth Meekes

"For Tommaso, my husband and friend. I love you and I like you, and that is saying a lot. For Max, proof that seven-year-old superheroes do exist. No other human on this planet has amazed or inspired me more."

-Candace Clark Trinchieri

"Many thanks to my dearest friends and family; salute to my co-authors and soul sisters at GBR; infinite love and gratitude to my whys: DJ, Jax, and Lil—I'm beyond blessed to grow through life with you. ♥"

-Krysta Lee

"Thank you to God, for all. Thanks to Krysta Lee, Sasha Hanson, and Golden Brick Road Publishing for this honor. Deepest love to Chris for always supporting me on my adventures. To our angels, Winston and Xavier, thank you for being the greatest stories of my life."

-Emanuela Martina Hall

"To our husbands, Chris and Justin, who have always been our biggest supporters in all we do. You both will forever be our go-to for unconditional love, comfort, and guidance. Thank you to all of our kids who fill our lives with purpose every day."

-Jaime Hayes & Marnie VandenBroek-Hookey

"For my parents who are my guardian angels, my husband who is the yin to my yang, and my children who are my forever teachers. I love you with all of my being."

-Lisa Kern

"Thank you to my family and friends who have supported me, especially my mom and dad, Izayah and Xander, and my mentors Seville and Rachaell Ko; thank you for always believing in me and showing me what's possible."

-Jessi Harris

"Thank you to my husband for pushing me to take a chance. My kids, for being my constant reminder to go after what you want in this life. And to my Community who fiercely shows up for me and one another."

-Susan Elstob

"A heartfelt thank you to all of the strong, beautiful women who inspired this chapter of my life: my coffee therapy Mamas, you know who you are, I love you all so much!"

-Sandy Casella

"For Brock, the glue that holds this crazy ship together. And for Elizabeth—we are better humans because of you, and we cannot wait to see who you choose to be."

-Abby Creek

"Thank you to my own mama. To my sister, Michelle, and my honorary ones Lisa and Adri. Aid, I know you're smiling down on me, and the head of my book club in Heaven!"

-Teresa Sturino Schiavone

"To my beautiful children—I love you, I love you more, I love you the mostest! Always remember you are BRAVER than you BELIEVE, STRONGER than you SEEM, SMARTER than you THINK, and LOVED more than you KNOW. XO Love Forever and Always, Mommy. ♥"

-Angel Kibble

"Thank you to my husband Khiem for being a great dad and partner, for always supporting me and my goals. Thank you to my daughters, Arya and Sydney for being the best teachers in life."

-Sonia Dong

"For Source, who shows me how life is to be truly lived. Ray, for holding space to spread my wings, and my kids, you are pure joy. I love you."

-Tamara Trotman

GOLDEN BRICK ROAD
PUBLISHING HOUSE

Link arms with us as we pave new paths to a better and more expansive world.

Golden Brick Road Publishing House (GBRPH) is a small, independently initiated boutique press created to provide social-innovation entrepreneurs, experts, and leaders a space in which they can develop their writing skills and content to reach existing audiences as well as new readers.

Serving an ambitious catalogue of books by individual authors, GBRPH also boasts a unique co-author program that capitalizes on the concept of "many hands make light work." GBRPH works with our authors as partners. Thanks to the value, originality, and fresh ideas we provide our readers, GBRPH books are now available in bookstores across North America.

We aim to develop content that effects positive social change while empowering and educating our members to help them strengthen themselves and the services they provide to their clients.

Iconoclastic, ambitious, and set to enable social innovation, GBRPH is helping our writers/partners make cultural change one book at a time.

Inquire today at www.goldenbrickroad.pub